Spinoza

OTHER TITLES IN THE ONEWORLD PHILOSOPHERS SERIES

Descartes, Harry M. Bracken, ISBN 1–85168–294–5
Kierkegaard, Michael Watts, ISBN 1–85168–317–8
Nietzsche, Robert Wicks, ISBN 1–85168–291–0
Sartre, Neil Levy, ISBN 1–85168–290–2
Wittgenstein, Avrum Stroll, ISBN 1–85168–293–7

OTHER PHILOSOPHY TITLES FROM ONEWORLD

Modern French Philosophy: From Existentialism to Postmodernism, Robert
   Wicks, ISBN 1–85168–318–6
Moral Relativism: A Short Introduction, Neil Levy, ISBN 1–85168–305–4
Political Philosophy: An Historical Introduction, Michael J. White,
   ISBN 1–85168–328–3

Spinoza

Richard H. Popkin

ONEWORLD PHILOSOPHERS

ONEWORLD
OXFORD

SPINOZA

Oneworld Publications
(Sales and Editorial)
185 Banbury Road
Oxford OX2 7AR
England
www.oneworld-publications.com

ISBN 1–85168–339–9

Cover design by the Bridgewater Book Company
Cover photograph of Baruch de Spinoza, Crayon engraving, 1762, by Jean Charles
François after Delhay © Photo: akg-images
Typeset by Saxon Graphics Ltd, Derby, UK
Printed and bound in China by Sun Fung Offset Binding Co. Ltd

Contents

Introduction

Baruch de Spinoza (1632–1677) was one of the most intriguing figures in the history of modern philosophy. His originality, audacity, and consistent rationality made him both hated and applauded by thinkers of all kinds. He was also just about the only person in modern philosophy whose personality had as much importance as his philosophy. Whereas other philosophers have been cited for their arguments, ideas, or theories, Spinoza has been offered as the epitome of what a true philosopher should be like as a person. Hence, Spinoza has been a unique figure among modern thinkers for the last three centuries, inspiring many different currents of thought and many different interpretations.

Harry Austryn Wolfson, the renowned Spinoza scholar of the first half of the twentieth century, said that Spinoza was the last of the medievals and the first of the moderns. On the one hand, Spinoza was still using some of the categories and conceptions of Arabic, Jewish, and Christian medieval thought. On the other hand, his great contribution lay in making a clean break with religious and theological philosophy. According to Wolfson, Spinoza was the first philosopher of modern times who required no axiom or premise based on revealed religious information. Descartes was still clinging to, or giving lip service to, a theological base for his new philosophy. Spinoza eliminated this and proceeded directly from a set of principles or axioms that had no theological content or import.[1]

Spinoza dispensed with any appeal to the supernatural to account for the world and how it operates. His brilliant system developed a complete picture of the world based solely on definitions and axioms and sought to explain *everything* in terms of the attributes of a non-supernatural God. The attributes that human beings could know were those of thought and extension and, through these, men can discover how the world operates, what it consists of, and the role of human beings in it. This conception enabled Spinoza to present a way in which people could find their goals in non-theological terms. This remarkable break with tradition was one of the most radical innovations in seventeenth-century thought and one that has continued to spawn interesting new understandings and insights in philosophy, ethics, and science.

His two major works, the *Tractatus Theologico-Politicus* (1670) and the *Ethics*, published posthumously in 1677, advanced his radical new conceptions. Subsequent philosophers have found much to contemplate and cogitate in these works, which are still very much in the main stream of philosophical discussion.

The picture that has been formed of Spinoza the thinker and Spinoza the moral agent was developed in the first biographical accounts of Spinoza: those by Pierre Bayle, Jean-Maximilien Lucas, and Johann Colerus, as well as those of the early German Enlightenment. Bayle, at the end of the seventeenth century, was compiling his massive *Dictionnaire historique et critique*. He intended to include important figures that had been misrepresented or left out of previous dictionaries. In the finished product, which first appeared in 1697, by far the longest article is that of Spinoza, being ten times the size of any other article. In fact, when taken out of its folio size and when the footnotes are incorporated it turns out to be a book of over 300 pages. Entitled

Het Leven de Spinoza, it was published as such in Dutch in 1697 by the publisher and bookseller Francis Halma.[2]

Bayle's article contains what is probably the first known biography of Spinoza but it is the Lucas biography that is generally called the earliest biography of Spinoza although there is no evidence that it existed before 1711–12. The Lucas biography, *La Vie de Spinosa*, first appeared in French along with a work called *L'esprit de M. Spinosa* or *Traité des trois Imposteurs*. Lucas is reported to have been a French Protestant refugee in Holland at the end of the seventeenth century who was part of a circle of spinozists. Nothing much is known of him even if he is the author of the early life of Spinoza.[3]

Johann Colerus was a Lutheran minister in The Hague who rented the very rooms that Spinoza lived in at the end of his life at the home of the painter Henrik van der Spyck. Colerus heard much about the philosopher from the landlord and decided to put together this material with whatever else he could find out about Spinoza from people in the Netherlands. His biography of Spinoza first appeared in 1705–6 and was quickly translated into many languages.[4]

Unfortunately, there is scant biographical material in the three original sources and not much more has come to light since. Thus, a lot of rumors, speculations, and fantasies have become mixed into the discussion of the life of the philosopher. We will try to unravel the various strands of Spinoza's short life in the pages that follow.

First, we will try to situate Spinoza in his historical context in the seventeenth century – a Jew born of Portuguese parents and raised in the Jewish community in Amsterdam, who was excommunicated from that group and then made his way in a quite different world, that of secular and Protestant society in the Netherlands. We will look at the ideas that appear in his earliest writings and in his fully developed ones, the *Tractatus* and the *Ethics*. We will then discuss his interaction with intellectuals of the time in the Netherlands and elsewhere and how his ideas came to be known to a wider audience. Finally, we will examine what sort of influence he has had over the last three centuries and more.

Chapter One

The Jewish community

Spinoza was born on November 24, 1632 in Amsterdam, the son of a Jewish Portuguese mother and father. Practicing Jews had been expelled from Spain in 1492 and a large number of them went to Portugal. In 1497 the Portuguese Jews were given a choice of accepting Christianity or being banished. Many of the Jews who remained both in Spain and Portugal, and who were forcibly converted to Christianity, secretly retained some of their Jewish affiliation. The Spanish and Portuguese Inquisitions were established to police the activities of the converted Jews (*conversos*) and to find out which of the *conversos* were *marranos* (people who still secretly practiced some aspect of Judaism). The Inquisition had no control over unconverted Jews, who were not considered heretics since they were not Christians, but it did have jurisdiction over the converted and baptized Jews. Spinoza's parents, who were crypto-Jews, or *marranos*, had been arrested in Portugal and charged with carrying on Jewish practices. They confessed and promised not to do it again and were released with fines and social disabilities, such as wearing a jacket on which was written the crimes that they had committed. This garment was also hung in the church so everyone would know their situation. If they were found backsliding again, the penalty could be death at the stake. Rather than risk this, Spinoza's parents fled from Iberia, going first to France and then to the Netherlands.[5]

From the early seventeenth century, a free Jewish society had developed in the northern Netherlands that attracted a stream of persecuted Sephardic Jews,* such as Spinoza's parents, from Spain, Portugal, Italy, and France. The territory was originally under the control of the Duke of Burgundy. In the early sixteenth century, when Charles V, who was the duke, became the king of Spain, control of the Netherlands passed to the Spanish crown. Charles's son, Philip, sought to unite the parts of his father's empire, including the Holy Roman Empire, Spain, Portugal, and the Netherlands, and to impose uniform laws on them. The northern Netherlands rebelled against Spanish inquisitorial persecution of Protestants in what is now Belgium. The rebellion began when the Spanish authorities tried to establish the Inquisition in the southern Netherlands. Centers of rebellion developed at Leiden and other northern cities. The Dutch, after a stubborn fight, managed to separate from Spanish control in 1568 and over the following years developed into an independent country consisting of seven provinces and the city of Amsterdam. After the rebellion, there was a problem of who was in charge of the Dutch territories. The highest official, the prince of Orange, was called the "stadholder," that is, the regent holding the territory for the monarch. This new nation had no clear sovereignty and the society developed as a compromise between the Calvinist House of Orange and the political forces in the various Dutch provinces.[6]

In 1619, the Synod of Dordrecht tried to establish a unified religion for the new state. However, it quickly became clear that there was a great split within the most powerful group, the Calvinists, and that there was enormous diversity of religious

---

*The Sephardim are Jews originally from Spain and Portugal. They are distinguished from the Jews of northern Europe, the Ashkenazim.

belief throughout the country. Some of this was the result of a large Catholic population in the southern part of the Netherlands – half the population was Catholic at the time – and another element was the various religious groups that either developed within the country or came from other lands. A book published in 1673 called *La Religion des Hollandois* (The Religion of the Dutch) claimed that the Netherlands was a religious madhouse, having over a hundred different religions functioning at the same time.[7] The orthodox Dutch Reform Church regarded itself as the established church and tried to control religious diversity through its edicts. However, the Netherlands was the economic and commercial center of colonial trade, with commerce passing through the country to the rest of Europe and beyond. Any attempt that interfered with commercial developments was resisted, such as the effort to impose religious uniformity. Most of the time the government would choose not to go along with attempts by the orthodox Calvinists to bring about religious conformity, finding it more beneficial for the economic development of the country to permit a wide diversity of religion. Although attempts to make Catholicism illegal did become law, this law was not enforced. Hence, the Netherlands became the most religiously tolerant part of Europe by default and not by a constitutional process. As traders from all over the world came to Amsterdam, various religious groups settled there and the Dutch authorities made minimal efforts to control and contain them.[8]

Many Dutch Protestants, like their English counterparts, the Puritans, saw the great change in their nation as part of the preparation for the Millennium, the second coming of Jesus and his thousand-year reign on earth. Dutch religious writers were excited about the theological significance of their military victory over the Catholic Spaniards, the rapid development of their new economy, and their success over the watery forces of nature (they had figured out how to clear the water off the land with the help of dyke construction, windmills and canals and how to make agriculture and commerce flourish in what had been a marshy terrain). Within this outlook, the role of the Jews took on a special significance. According to the Book of Revelation, the Jews would convert freely and spiritually to Christianity as the penultimate step before the return of Jesus. As a result, the Jewish community in the Netherlands was cultivated by Protestant leaders in the hope that signs of their conversion would soon become apparent.[9]

Early in the seventeenth century, the Dutch political authorities also began to take notice of Spanish and Portuguese Jews living in the Dutch Republic. They first regarded them as cohorts of their Spanish enemies because they spoke Spanish. When they discovered they had also been persecuted by the Spaniards they agreed to let them carry on their religious life in the Netherlands. Although the Jewish community in Amsterdam at the time was operating in a Christian society, it was not under the usual rules and regulations that governed Jews in other Christian lands such as Germany or Italy. The question of what status the Jews had was partially worked out in some unwritten regulations of 1616 that made it legal for Jews to have their own private religious services as long as they did not commit blasphemy or annoy their Christian neighbors. In the accepted rules, the Jews were told not to write anything against Christianity and not to publish anything that would cause scandal, whatever that might be. The Dutch authorities seemed to have had only a vague idea of the new world they were entering into by allowing a non-Christian group to have a legally protected status. In the course of the next fifty years, the Jewish community and the surrounding Dutch Christian community had to test what was acceptable to each side. The Jews were not encased in a ghetto but could live wherever they pleased. This led to social mixing that was unusual for its time. Some of the discussions indicate that the authorities and the Dutch society were upset by sexual interaction and by certain kinds of economic activities, including extravagant memorial monuments and ostentatious home ornamentation.

But these discussions also show that they were favorably impressed by how the Jewish community carried on its religious activities except when these became too boisterous.[10]

The question of exactly what Jews could or could not do was taken up by the distinguished legal authority Hugo Grotius, who was asked to formulate some laws that would define how Jews could function in a Christian society, albeit a diverse Christian society. Grotius proposed a moderate plan with some restrictions. But before his plan could be adopted, Grotius himself had to flee religious persecution.[11]

In the end, the Dutch authorities made an informal agreement with the Spanish and Portuguese Jews that they could live openly in Amsterdam and other cities as long as they did not cause scandal or allow any of their religious brethren to become public charges. The Jewish community grew quickly. Its members were mainly *marranos* who had very little training in Judaism. The community basically created its own version of Jewish practices and beliefs, mingling freely with other religious groups. At first, they shared a building in which to worship with some English dissident Protestant groups, albeit, of course, at different times. They encouraged their neighbors to see how they practice their religion and Amsterdam soon became the only place in Europe where Christians could mingle freely with Jews in their synagogues and discuss their differing views. The Jewish community developed educational and cultural institutions to keep up their Iberian heritage and to guide their religious beliefs and practices. Services were conducted in Spanish and Portuguese and there were classes teaching more or less the same subjects as were taught in Catholic schools in Spain and Portugal.

Many of the Iberian Jews who came to the Netherlands were quickly engaged in international commerce. In the first half of the seventeenth century, Amsterdam became the center for the transport of goods from overseas empires into Europe and the center of international banking. Many Sephardic Jews took part in the Dutch economic miracle of the time and became wealthy.

The leaders of the community were both the important commercial laymen and the rabbis. The power rested with the laymen (the *parnassim*) who appointed the rabbis and made the decisions for the community. In the seventeenth and eighteenth centuries, the community carefully protected the status of the *parnassim* as the ultimate authority. When rabbis from other parts of the world came and tried to get them to adopt certain views, the community would insist that only the *parnassim* could decide these matters. During this period the rabbis were self-selected, with little formal training, and treated as employees to be hired and fired at the will of the *parnassim*. To enforce any religious claims, the rabbis needed the backing of the *parnassim*, who were usually the wealthiest members of the group. Spinoza's father, Michael Espinosa, served for a couple of years as a *parnas*.

Anecdotal evidence suggests that informal debates between Christians and Jews and criticisms of each other's religion started occurring in the streets of Amsterdam. Also, after 1617, there are indications that criticisms of Christianity by Jews were being circulated in manuscript and that a professor at Leiden was attempting to refute these views. Elijah Montalto, the Jewish physician to Queen Marie de Medici of France, had written a critique of the Christian interpretation of Isaiah 53 and also a controversial work opposing his, Montalto's, views to those of some Catholic theologians.

A different kind of anti-Christian work came on the scene sometime in the late 1620s. A Lithuanian Caraite rabbi, Abraham Isaac of Troki (1533–1594), had written a work in Hebrew in 1592 called *Chizzuk Emunah* (The Fortification of the Faith).[12] The manuscript is a very forceful attack on basic Christian concepts and arguments for the Christian interpretation of the Old Testament. The work appeared in several languages in Amsterdam – Spanish, Portuguese, French, and Dutch – and soon became very popular.[13] Technically, it did not break the original understanding that the Jews would not write anti-Christian material in Amsterdam since this was written elsewhere and the wide distribution of the Troki manuscript suggests there was no effort to suppress it.[14]

Domestic anti-Christian works start appearing at the end of the 1650s. The first is the monumental writing of over four hundred pages by Rabbi Saul Levi Morteira, the chief rabbi of Amsterdam during Spinoza's time, entitled *Providencia de Dios con Israel.* This was apparently written in 1659, a year before his demise. It is a massive, learned attack on Christian theology and dogma. Many manuscripts of it exist, some elegantly illustrated, some, like the Troki manuscript, looking like medieval illuminated manuscripts. In addition, Morteira gave sermons from the time he became a rabbi in Amsterdam. Recently 550 of his sermons have been discovered in Budapest by Professor Marc Saperstein, who is gradually analyzing them and making them available. These are Hebrew copies made by Morteira himself of sermons he gave in Portuguese. In these, there is a recurring theme of attacking Catholicism because of what it had done to the Spanish and Portuguese Jews and of showing the advantages of Judaism over the religion of Portugal and Spain. In the work written at the end of his life, the attack broadens to include Calvinism as well and to challenge the central theses of Christianity and to answer Christian anti-Jewish works such as those by Pablo de Santa Maria and Sixtus of Sienna.[15]

A few years later, two more Amsterdam Jewish intellectuals produced large anti-Christian writings – Isaac Orobio da Castro and Moses Raphael d'Aguilar. Orobio and d'Aguilar discussed their opposition to Christianity and their worries about deviant Jewish views.[16] Orobio said on the flyleaf of a manuscript of his work that still exists in Amsterdam that he did not publish it for fear of causing scandal but that he sent it to the Jesuits in Brussels who liked it very much. Orobio's explanation may account for why the others also did not publish. But perhaps a more interesting question is why they started writing these strong attacks on Christianity from 1659 onward. Such literature does not exist at any other time in Jewish history and each of these polemics was to have an important afterlife in the Enlightenment when they became available to non-Jewish readers.[17]

It was evidently acceptable to the Dutch Christian community that the synagogue could have open discussions in the sermons criticizing Christianity provided these were predominantly directed against Catholicism, the common enemy of the Dutch Calvinists and the Spanish and Portuguese Jews. As long as nothing was said about Jesus they avoided committing blasphemy on this score. An analysis of some of Morteira's sermons indicates that there he used a sort of crypto language, whereby the former Christian, now Jewish, members of the audience would get a message that might escape other Christian listeners. In this way, the preacher could say things about Christianity obliquely which, if said directly, would have been blasphemous.[18] Orobio de Castro also took part in a public disputation with the Protestant leader Philip van Limborch, a liberal Calvinist. This debate was published in 1687 and again in the early eighteenth century and attracted much attention; the volume is cited fairly often.

Probably the most virulent anti-Christian writing of the time is the work called the *Porta Veritatis*. It is not mentioned in any of the literature about anti-Christian writings of the time in the Netherlands. It surfaces for the first time we know of when Rabbi Menasseh ben Israel, a teacher of Spinoza, sold a copy of it in 1655 or 1656 to the Regius professor of Hebrew at Cambridge, Ralph Cudworth. Menasseh was then in England negotiating the possible readmission of the Jews. Cudworth, who had just met him, asked him why he did not accept Christianity. Menasseh showed him this manuscript, the *Porta Veritatis*, in Latin and sold it to him for ten pounds. Cudworth spent a good deal of effort trying to refute it and his unfinished efforts are still in the British Library. He also complained to the authorities about it. It was willed by him to Bishop Richard Kidder of Bath and Wells, who said it was so awful that nobody but a true and believing Christian should be allowed to look at it and had it put under lock and key at the Bodleian Library in Oxford.[19]

While most of the other members of the Jewish community had been born in Christian lands as Catholics, and in some cases Protestants, and reverted to Judaism when they got to Amsterdam, young Spinoza was from the first generation of Jews born in Amsterdam who had never suffered from anti-Jewish regulations. He had learned a little about the persecutions in Spain from his parents and sermons in the synagogue. Did he also learn some of his later biblical criticism from the anti-Christian views being circulated in the Jewish community? Though he never refers to any of the unpublished anti-Christian polemics, similar arguments to those of Troki and others turn up in Spinoza's critique of modern Bible interpreters. Spinoza's argument for the unity of substance is close to Troki's arguments against the doctrine of the Trinity. More relevant is that Spinoza's evaluation of some of the biblical passages about divine activities strikes similar notes to Troki's resistance to anthropological readings by Christians of his time. It is hard to imagine that Spinoza could have grown up in Amsterdam without coming into contact with this literature and without discussing it with others.

In the period leading up to Spinoza's break with the Jewish community the records of the synagogue indicate that a lot of deviant behavior went on and that the efforts to set up a rigid society were not working at all. Congregants had to be told repeatedly that they should give up attending Christian church services, that they should not eat non-Kosher food, and things of this sort. In 1651, Isaac Lopes Suasso moved to Amsterdam and joined the synagogue. He was a merchant from Belgium who had lived his life up until then as a New Christian and his brother was professor of Catholic theology at Bordeaux. There is no evidence that Lopes Suasso was a *marrano*, secretly practicing Judaism. His decision to move to Amsterdam seems to have been guided by economic forces, moving his business from Antwerp to Amsterdam and marrying the daughter of Abraham de Pinto, who happened to be the richest Jewish merchant in

Amsterdam. Lopes Suasso was made secretary treasurer of the group in 1653. The by-laws stated that one could only be a *parnas* after three years of membership but this was overlooked in Lopes Suasso's case. He was secretary treasurer during the period of Spinoza's break with the synagogue. There is nothing in what we presently know to show that he was actively engaged in the problems caused by young Spinoza. Instead, we find from the records that he was very busy dealing with two of the biggest social issues in the Jewish community of the time. The first was the hundreds and hundreds of Spanish Jews who had to be resettled after they had been driven out of Brazil. They had established a colony in 1642 at Recife when the Dutch controlled the territory and this colony was extremely prosperous until recaptured by the Portuguese in 1654. This created a large number of wealthy refugees. Some found new homes in the Caribbean; some became the first Jews in New Amsterdam and Rhode Island; but most returned to the Netherlands. They had to be re-established and reintegrated into the community. The rabbinical leader of the group in Brazil, Isaac Aboab de Fonseca, became the second-in-command at the Amsterdam synagogue and was also given the task of establishing a kabbalistic yeshiva in Amsterdam.

A quite different social problem had been created by the disruption of Jewish life in Eastern Europe. The Swedish army invaded Poland and captured some of the major territories where Jews lived, such as Vilna. Thousands of Jews fled eastward across northern Germany into the Netherlands. These Jews, Ashkenazim, came mainly as penniless refugees. The Jewish community of Amsterdam understood its commitment to making sure no Jews became public charges, so one finds in the synagogue records of Lopes Suasso that he was arranging various *ad hoc* solutions for the Ashkenazi refugees, such as resettling them in Germany and finding boats to take them out of Amsterdam.[20] Indications of the extent of the problem can be seen in some of Rembrandt's drawings of the time with poor

Jews in rags depicted outside and around the synagogue in Amsterdam. By Spinoza's time, half the members of the congregation were Ashkenazim. Their needs and attitudes were treated cursorily and they took no part in the management or running of the synagogue. The Ashkenazim were generally poorer and dependent on the good will and largesse of the richer Iberian Jews. This dichotomy became evident with the Ashkenazim being relegated to jobs such as cleaning out the synagogue, washing the windows, and moving the furniture, while the Sephardim took care of the education of the young, the poetry and dramatic societies, and contacts with the outside world. A few years later, the Ashkenazic Jews established their own synagogue across the street and the original congregation, from then on, was dedicated just to the Sephardic group. They built the Grand Synagogue, which is still standing, in the 1660s and it was dedicated in 1672 with great ceremony throughout Amsterdam. It was, at the time, the largest building in Amsterdam and still is the largest synagogue in Western Europe.

The above picture of how the Amsterdam synagogue developed provides the setting for the Spinoza drama. The main focus of the synagogue was to provide a community for Portuguese and Spanish exiles who had come to Amsterdam, to give them an opportunity to continue the cultural life of Iberia, and to adopt and live by some of the Jewish traditions. Furthermore, as we have seen, the two main problems of the reintegration and resettlement of the Sephardic refugees from Brazil and the problem of dealing with the poverty-stricken Ashkenazim fleeing from Eastern Europe seem to be the main focus of the treasurer's problems of the time. Spinoza only enters into Lopes Suasso's notes when he records the actual expulsion of Spinoza. The picture we have drawn of the activities of the Amsterdam synagogue indicate that it was not particularly repressive or doctrinaire. It seemed to allow a wide variety of activities and attitudes among its members, old and young. We do not know much about what training it provided to one of its most brilliant students, Baruch de Spinoza. We do know that he was excommunicated in 1656 so we have to look backwards to try to discover what led to this drastic outcome.

Early intellectual life in Amsterdam

In July 1656 Spinoza was excommunicated from the Amsterdam synagogue, charged with holding horrendous views and abysmal practices. Scholars have been trying for three and a half centuries to divine what he must have done to bring about this sort of treatment. Although there are no records that provide much of a clue, the intellectual development of Spinoza has generally been interpreted through this event. Many theories have been offered about his education leading up to the excommunication and foreshadowing his great philosophical progress thereafter. We know that he was an excellent student in the synagogue schools and had won a prize and that he was selected to teach some of the younger students. Beyond this we can only hypothesize.

The inventory we have of Spinoza's library, which was compiled after his death, has only 161 volumes, less than half of which are on philosophy or theology. It is a very spartan collection for somebody who had taken on such vast intellectual undertakings as Spinoza had. He owned works by Aristotle, Seneca, Cicero, Maimonides, Descartes, Hobbes, and Francis Bacon, among others.[21] We do not know if Spinoza had many more volumes that have been lost but when could they have been lost since he died at such a young age? He may have borrowed texts but such information has not come down to us. Spinoza, unlike contemporaries such as Leibniz, was not building up his interpretation of the world by studying previous constructions and building on them. It is more a unique effort to get beyond what previous thinkers had been able to do. Spinoza stresses in the appendix to Book one of the *Ethics* that what he is doing is only possible because of the reintroduction of mathematics into philosophical thinking. As he makes clear in that context, it is through the mathematical description of events that we are able to tell that events are not occurring because of purposes in the world: the whole teleological description of nature can be set aside and the world can be then interpreted according to what Spinoza would call the true philosophy. This very bold move not only emancipated philosophers, but also made them independent of what had come before them.

Spinoza's library also includes a few books of Jewish interest. We do not know precisely when he acquired these and so any interpretation of their influence upon him is just conjectural. One of these books is a sixteenth-century Spanish edition of the work of Leone Ebreo, *Dialoghi di Amore* (The Dialogues of Love). The author was the son of the last leader of the Spanish Jews prior to the expulsion of the Jews from Spain in 1492, Don Isaac Abravanel. The work – a Neoplatonic presentation, a format that was extremely popular at the time – appeared in Italian in the first part of the sixteenth century. It contains two of Spinoza's great goals in intellectual life: that of seeing the world in the aspect of eternity and that of achieving the intellectual love of God. We also know that Spinoza read the Spanish Jewish anti-Aristotelian philosopher Hasdai Crescas at some early stage and used some of his arguments. Harry A. Wolfson, Warren Harvey, and others have examined medieval or Renaissance texts that we know Spinoza was acquainted with.[22] Besides the obvious indebtedness of Spinoza to Maimonides, they also show how important Crescas and Leone Ebreo were in the formation of

Spinoza's philosophy. Wolfson showed that Spinoza used material from Crescas in the *Ethics*. A great deal of Neoplatonic material that appears in Spinoza can be accounted for from his acquaintance with Leone Ebreo's masterwork. Also, Spinoza's knowledge of, and use of, arguments and philosophical claims of Solomon Ibn Gabirol could have come from Leone Ebreo or Leone's use and knowledge of Ficino's Platonism. A further influence that is hard to assess is that of the philosophical kabbalist Abraham Cohen Herrera. His work, *Puerto de Cielo*, circulated in manuscript in Spanish and an abridged Hebrew version, was published in 1655 by Rabbi Isaac Aboab. Spinoza knew some key terms from Herrera's system and employs them in his *Ethics*. Presumably, Spinoza could have read either the Spanish manuscripts or the Hebrew abridgement.

Another important intellectual influence on the young Spinoza was that of Cartesianism. It is of interest, and even of some importance, to try to assess when and how Spinoza first came to know of Cartesianism and, therefore, when he became involved with modern thought. Descartes's philosophy had only appeared in Latin so the question becomes, when did Spinoza learn Latin? Two early biographies of Spinoza speak of him studying Latin with a former Jesuit, Franciscus van den Enden. The texts are not clear as to when he began his studies. Some of the Spinoza literature contends that Latin would have been a rare language for Jews to study because it was the priest's language. However, because most of the members of the Jewish community were former *marranos* who had studied in Catholic or Protestant institutions in Spain, Portugal, France, or Italy, Latin would have been a language with which many of them were familiar. Rabbi Saul Levi Morteira had been the scribe for a Latin medical treatise of Doctor Montalto. Juan de Prado, who was a close associate of Spinoza in 1655–6, had received doctoral degrees in medicine and theology in Spain and, hence, would have been well versed in Latin. Orobio de Castro, the leading intellectual of the community, was a graduate of the University of

Salamanca and had taught at the University of Toulouse. He continued reading the Bible in Latin all of his life and it was in the same language that he wrote a refutation of Spinoza. All of this suggests that knowledge of Latin was not a problem. A recent study by Jonathan Israel suggests that Spinoza must have known Latin from an early age because of his great mastery of Cartesian philosophy, but he may have been able to accomplish this in just a couple of years.[23] We do not know whether Spinoza started studying Latin before his excommunication or after and what years he actually studied Latin with the French radical deist van den Enden. It seems plausible that a bright student of Spanish Portuguese background would not have great difficulty in starting to learn Latin. So, Spinoza could have started his Latin education before his excommunication and continued it later on. Spinoza's library contained books in Latin, although we do not know when he obtained them.

One item in Spinoza's library was Isaac La Peyrère's *Prae-Adamitae* (Men Before Adam). It was only published in Latin in 1655 in five different editions and it was banned at the end of the year and never reprinted. Spinoza used it extensively in the *Tractatus Theologico-Politicus*, so we can presume that he was able to read it early in his career. The author of *Prae-Adamitae* was a French Protestant, possibly a *marrano* from Bordeaux. He had written his work much earlier and only decided to publish it when Queen Christina of Sweden urged him to do so and offered to pay for it. In his book La Peyrère challenged the accuracy of present copies of the Bible and insisted that the best evidence would indicate that the Bible is the history of the Jews and not the history of mankind. His book was one of the few denounced and banned in the Netherlands and, by the end of 1655, La Peyrère was being condemned as a Jew and a godless atheist. He was arrested in Belgium, and nobody was able to get him liberated, even though he was the secretary of the very powerful prince of Condé, the second ranking nobleman in France. Word was sent that he could be released if he promised to convert to

Catholicism and apologize personally to the pope. La Peyrère, as a good courtier, went to Rome and made his apologies to Pope Alexander VII and said that his errors were due to his religious upbringing. He was taught, as a Calvinist, to use his reason as the basis for his faith. He would now give up his reason and accept whatever the pope told him. He wrote a most unconvincing apology and then retired to France where he became the librarian of the pious order of the Oratorians.[24]

La Peyrère's case was notorious at the time. Five editions of his book came out in Amsterdam in spite of the ban on it and it was claimed there was even a sect called the Pre-Adamites. One presumes that a bright, alert student like Spinoza must have been loaned the book or have been interested in the career of the author. As we shall see in chapter 6, many of Spinoza's critical points about the Bible probably come from La Peyrère.

Another notorious case that has been linked to the young Spinoza is that of the earlier heretic Uriel da Costa. There is a nineteenth-century portrait of Da Costa holding little Spinoza on his knee, one rebel preparing another for combat, and much has been written about whether Spinoza's radical views about Judaism derived from those of Da Costa. Da Costa was a Portuguese *marrano* who was a church official in Portugal. He fled to Amsterdam in the second decade of the seventeenth century with his mother, two brothers, and other relatives. The male members of the family became involved in various bureaucratic functions in the Jewish community and came into contact with Spinoza's father, Michael. Uriel, formally Gabriel, very quickly started criticizing the kind of religion being practiced by the Jews in Amsterdam. While still in Portugal, he had come to believe in some sort of pure, original Judaism that he encountered in the Bible and, consequently, found the Amsterdam version full of things that came from the rabbinical tradition and not from Holy Writ. He aggressively attacked many forms of Talmudic Judaism, coming into conflict with members of the Jewish congregation because of his insistence that Judaism is, in truth, the views of the Sadducees and not of the Pharisees and that the Oral Law has no status. He also maintained that Judaism did not advocate the immortality of the soul. He not only argued for these positions but also wrote a lengthy work *Exame das tradições phariseas* (Examination of Pharisaic Traditions) in 1624 defending his claims. All copies of his book were ordered to be destroyed; he was arrested by the civil authorities because his book attacked both Christianity and Judaism, and given a substantial fine.[25]

Uriel da Costa had been excommunicated by the synagogue a year earlier in 1623. The excommunication order stated that no member of the Amsterdam Jewish community could give him food or sustenance or be in contact with him. His brothers disowned him and refused to have anything more to do with him. However, his mother maintained close contact and continued to live in the same house as her heretical son. For several years Da Costa tried to live outside the Jewish community without joining any other religious group. However, the isolation and ostracism proved too much for him and he sought ways to get himself readmitted into the synagogue. Finally, he was allowed to rejoin but had to undergo a severe punishment. But, soon after, he began to voice the same questions and arguments that had led to his excommunication and was expelled once more. In despair, we are told, he committed suicide, but not before writing a fiery autobiography defending the right to independent opinions. He is supposed to have cried out that he did not want to be a monkey among monkeys but, rather, a man among men.

We know nothing about the public reaction to Da Costa's case at the time except for one mention by a German pastor Müller, who either heard of it or was present. Otherwise, it is not mentioned by Spinoza or any member of the congregation or any of the Christian philosemites who attended the synagogue. Da Costa only came to public notice in 1687 when his autobiography was published as an appendix to the disputation between

Orobio de Castro and Philip van Limborch concerning the truth of the Christian religion.[26] Orobio died before the text of the debate was published and had nothing to do with its editing and there is no indication that he had anything to say about Da Costa. In fact, Orobio was the only member of the Spanish Portuguese congregation that wrote against Spinoza. His response is purely philosophical.[27] Nobody seems to have connected the Da Costa story, which became public this way, with Spinoza, who was emerging as one of the most important and controversial modern thinkers.

The provenance of the manuscript that was printed in 1687 was, we are told, a manuscript that Philip van Limborch's father-in-law had received. The manuscript, which still exists, is in consecutive order even though portions of Da Costa's life are left out.[28] It would seem to have been copied from an edited version that we do not now have. It is interesting that once Da Costa's autobiography appeared this seemed to provide a context that helped explain Spinoza's emergence. Prior to the 1687 publication, Spinoza's radical thoughts had been traced back to his Latin teacher, Van den Enden, as there did not seem to be anything in the Jewish tradition in Amsterdam that could have produced a rebel like Spinoza. The dates indicate that Spinoza should have been present at the punishment of Da Costa when the latter was readmitted into the Jewish community but neither Spinoza nor any other member of the congregation mentions the matter. Unfortunately, we have no evidence that it had any influence in the Jewish community or outside and whether it influenced Spinoza or not is, so far, impossible to determine.

Steven Nadler, in his admirable biography of Spinoza, has pointed out that at the time of Da Costa's rebellion several of the rabbis, including Chief Rabbi Morteira, Menasseh ben Israel, and Isaac Aboab, wrote works justifying beliefs in the immortality of the soul. Since these same rabbis were around when Spinoza rebelled, Nadler contends that the principle reason for Spinoza's excommunication is that they saw the same issue arising and did not want it to get out of hand again. The rabbis who fought against Da Costa fifteen or sixteen years earlier did not want another outbreak of the same kind and so quickly got rid of Spinoza.[29] However, Menasseh ben Israel was in England and not Amsterdam at the time of Spinoza's excommunication and there is no evidence that he had any opinion of what was going on in Amsterdam. Morteira was busily writing his work against Christian apologetics. His sermons of the time do not mention anything about Spinoza or Da Costa, nor do those of Rabbi Aboab. Therefore, there is no evidence that the issue that galvanized the Jewish community against Uriel da Costa was also the motivation to expel Spinoza at a later date.

If the Da Costa episode had been known generally one would expect that some of the early Spinoza literature that criticized the Jewish community would have brought this up. The sad tale told in Da Costa's autobiography was immediately taken up by Pierre Bayle in his article "Acosta," an important statement of Bayle's tolerance and of his theory about the relation between skepticism and religion. From then on, it was told and retold as an illustration of how intolerant the Portuguese Jewish congregation was. But no comparison is made by Bayle of Da Costa with Spinoza, even though Bayle must have known that Spinoza would be the major figure in his *Dictionnaire*. Furthermore, in his long article on Spinoza, Bayle describes Spinoza's early life with no mention of Da Costa. He comments that Spinoza got into many disagreements with the religious authorities but there is no indication that there was any attempt to connect him with the previous heretic.

The so-called earliest biography attributed to Jean-Maximillien Lucas has a lot of sordid detail about how nasty Rabbi Morteira was to Spinoza. Nothing is said at all to indicate that this is the way freethinkers were treated at the synagogue, as in the case of Da Costa. Additionally, in the earliest printed biography of Spinoza by the Lutheran minister Johannes Colerus, there is no mention of Da Costa. Colerus got his information from Spinoza's landlord, Hendrik Van der Spyck, and from various people who had known Spinoza. He could not find anyone who had been present at the denunciation of Spinoza and, therefore, obtained his information about the excommunication from Christian Hebraic accounts of what Jewish punishments were like in ancient and medieval times.

I think we are still left with big questions as to whether the Da Costa affair foreshadowed, influenced, or played any role in Spinoza's affairs. I believe Nadler is probably right that the rabbis would remember, especially if they wrote books arguing against Da Costa's views of the immortality of the soul. But if they did remember they did not seem to associate the previous renegade with the present one. In addition, none of Spinoza's biographers connected his excommunication with Da Costa.

Young Spinoza absorbed various threads of previous Jewish philosophers as well as some of the current ideas in the broader philosophical world. It is hard to tell how much of this background material he had taken into his view when he was twenty or twenty-one. People looking for explanations for his excommunication, which will be the subject of the next chapter, try to find views from his Jewish heritage and from the current philosophical discussions of the time that could have led Spinoza to be a heretic. Unfortunately, we do not have enough material to be able to say with any precision how much he relied on one set of views or another and the excommunication document just said he had horrible views but did not specify what those views were.

Chapter Three

The excommunication

The pronouncement on July 27, 1656 of the excommunication of Spinoza is often seen as a crucial turning point in his life and intellectual development. However, to this day we are not sure why he was excommunicated and what this actually entailed at the time. We have no records concerning his case and no testimonies by himself or anyone else as to what actually occurred. The excommunication decree (*herem*) denounces Spinoza for his horrendous sentiments and practices but gives no details. It pours out hundreds of curses upon him from the Old Testament and says that no member of the Jewish community should give him any food, drink, shelter, or solace, and that members of the community should not read anything he has written. There is no indication, however, that he had written anything up to this point.

The statement of the *herem* makes it look as if the community despised Spinoza and wanted to get rid of him as fast as possible. Yet, in their covering statement, it is said that the leaders (presumably *parnassim* and rabbis) had tried to reason with him and had offered him a sizeable pension if he would stay within the community and would appear in the synagogue on High Holidays and not make any fuss. They claim that it was only after Spinoza refused this offer the strong denunciation was made, which indicates that, no matter what he had done, the community would have put up with him on fairly amiable terms. In some of the Spinoza literature, such as the early biography by Lucas, the picture is given of Chief Rabbi Morteira as being incensed by Spinoza's criticisms of Judaism – so incensed that he forced the excommunication. However, as we now know, the rabbis could only recommend the punishment; it was the *parnassim* alone who had the power to excommunicate.

After Spinoza became well-known, people interested in his career tried to find out what happened on the day of the excommunication. They were unable to find anyone who had been a witness at the synagogue. This is probably due to the fact that the excommunication statement seems to have been read out in a small council chamber adjacent to the synagogue and was only witnessed by the *parnassim* and the rabbis. Spinoza himself was not present, having already moved outside the Jewish community. We are told that a messenger had to be sent to Spinoza to present him with a copy of the *herem*.[30] Spinoza himself never mentions the content of the excommunication statement. Instead, when asked why he left Amsterdam, he told people that he had been attacked outside a theater and that somebody had put a knife through his coat. He kept the coat until the end of his life and showed it to people with the hole still in it.[31] He did not, apparently, keep a copy of the denunciation. According to his inventory of materials that he possessed at the time of his death, there was a work called *The Apology*, presumed to be an answer in Spanish to the charges made against him. Both Bayle and Lucas mention that such an item existed but no copy of it has yet been found. Hence, we can only guess at what he might have said.

Before offering some speculation as to why Spinoza may have been excommunicated, it should be noted that this practice was not rare among the members of the Amsterdam congregation. In its first hundred years, this community pronounced *herems* against over two hundred and eighty people. These were usually to force people to pay their dues, to carry through marriage contracts, or because of adultery. One person was excommunicated for buying a kosher chicken from an Ashkenazi butcher rather than a Sephardic one. Menasseh ben Israel was excommunicated for one day for insulting a member of the *parnassim*. In almost all cases the excommunicated party was allowed to make up for his or her fault by paying fines, performing certain actions, or promising better behavior.[32] There are only a handful of ideological cases. The earliest, from 1617, concerned a person named David Farrar who caused a lot of consternation with his heterodox remarks and views. The young congregation did not know how to get rid of him when he refused to stop so they sent a delegation to Venice headed by the recently arrived Rabbi Saul Levi Morteira to solicit advice from learned Jewish scholars there. Morteira himself was a Venetian, believed to have studied with Rabbi Leone de Modena, and presumably would have had contacts among the Venetian rabbinate. The group from Amsterdam was given a formal statement of excommunication with all the curses and this just had to be filled out for the particular case at issue.[33] It is this *herem* that presumably was used in 1617 against Farrar and later for the excommunications of Uriel da Costa, Spinoza, and some eighteenth-century heretics. Hence, the statement cannot be taken personally as the special denunciation of young Spinoza.

A clue as to why Spinoza was expelled from the Jewish community is that, at the same time that he was excommunicated, a friend of his who shared his heterodox philosophy, Juan de Prado, apologized to the community and said he would withdraw those views that troubled them. Prado, who was much older than Spinoza, had been a medical and theological student in Spain and the doctor to a Spanish cardinal. He became worried about his possible arrest in Spain and therefore, on a trip to Rome with his clerical employer, he escaped with his family. They first went north to Hamburg and then to Amsterdam.

In the Jewish community Prado and Spinoza both taught Sabbath school to young children and they seem to have become good intellectual companions. They shared a critical view of biblical Judaism, apparently having doubts as to whether all the events described in the Bible literally took place. They seem to have taken over some of Isaac La Peyrère's biblical criticisms and explained them to their young students.[34] Charges were made against Prado, Spinoza, and another teacher, Daniel Ribera, a former Spanish monk who had joined the Jewish community. These three were accused of leading their students astray, suggesting that the Bible was not the history of the world, that Chinese history was independent of biblical history, and so on. Later, Prado was attacked for writing a book on why the law of nature takes precedence over the Law of Moses. A classmate of his from Spain, Isaac Orobio de Castro, said that Prado had already become a deist in Spain, whatever that might have meant at the time. But Prado had a wife and children who were being supported by the Amsterdam Jewish community and he did not, therefore, have the luxury of being able to take the stance Spinoza did and so repented.[35] However, the following year, Prado was excommunicated and left the Jewish community for good.

If one reason for the excommunication may have been Spinoza's critical views about the Bible, other suggestions have been made and explored. Spinoza, by the time of the excommunication, was involved with some radical Protestants. He was also exploring new philosophical ideas, especially those of René Descartes.[36] It has also been suggested recently that Spinoza was in deep legal trouble with the tax authorities and that this was causing disputes between him and the Jewish community.[37] These and many other possibilities have been raised and explored without coming to any satisfactory conclusion. I will briefly discuss the evidence for some of this.

It has been argued by Lewis Feuer that Spinoza's association with radical Christians may have caused difficulties within the Jewish community.[38] While a vendor of tropical fruits, Spinoza became a friend of Jarig Jelles, a Collegiant whose produce stand was next to the one Spinoza had along the harbor, and he remained close to him throughout his life. The Collegiants were a creedless, somewhat mystical, group that met as a spiritual brotherhood. The leader of the Amsterdam Collegiants was Adam Boreel, a Hebraist who was much involved with English millenarians and with Menasseh ben Israel. Boreel had become involved in the project of Rabbi Judah Leon to build an exact replica of Solomon's Temple. Since Solomon's Temple was supposed to be a microcosm of the universe, presumably Rabbi Judah Leon's model would allow the study or understanding of the whole cosmos. Boreel financed the work of this model and even had the rabbi and his family living in his house. Boreel learned Portuguese so that he could work more easily with the rabbi.[39]

After this venture, which resulted in a portable model that was on display next to the synagogue in Amsterdam for many years, Boreel became actively involved in a Judeo-Christian project – that of publishing the Mishnah with Hebrew vowel points and footnotes. Rabbi Judah Leon put in the vowel points, Boreel inserted the footnotes, and Menasseh ben Israel was the publisher. This project, which was completed in 1646, was followed by an uncompleted effort to put out the Mishnah in Spanish and, later, in Latin. In view of Boreel's interest in fostering Jewish-Christian learning projects and his involvement with several of the rabbis, it is hard to believe that Spinoza's friendship with some of the other Collegiants in Amsterdam would have raised any hackles.[40]

Another radical Protestant group with whom Spinoza was apparently involved was the Quakers. This English religious movement, which burst on to the scene in 1652, crossed the Channel and set up an Amsterdam base in 1656. One of their leaders, James Naylor, had claimed to be the messiah and replicated Jesus' entry into Jerusalem in the English city of Bristol. His followers called him the king of the Jews and sang "Hosanna in the Highest" as he proceeded into the city on the back of a donkey. He was arrested, charged with blasphemy, and tried by the English parliament. Oliver Cromwell defended him but, nonetheless, he was convicted and severely punished. His followers and sympathizers fled, some of them going to Amsterdam. There, they became involved with other dissident religious groups and with the Jews. They attended synagogue services and tried to convince the Jews to join them. Shortly after his excommunication, Spinoza was introduced to the Quaker leader in the Netherlands, William Ames, and was described by Peter Serrarius as a "Jew who by the Jews hath been cast out." Serrarius, a radical Protestant merchant, had also been involved with Menasseh ben Israel and soon became a patron of Spinoza.[41]

Spinoza's relationship with the Quakers would hardly be a reason for his excommunication since the Quaker Samuel Fisher happily explained how the Jews in the synagogue liked to discuss matters with him and how he treated synagogue services as a Quaker meeting and began speaking whenever the spirit moved him. He was asked by the Jewish leaders to restrain himself until the services were over and then they would be glad to talk to him at length. Fisher boasted that he spent three or four amiable hours in their homes after the services.[42] There were all sorts of friendly interchanges between Jewish and Christian leaders in the 1650s. Rabbi Nathan Shapira from Jerusalem dined and discussed central religious points with Peter Serrarius and his friends,[43] Serrarius made kabbalistic calculations (*gematria*) with rabbis at the synagogue, and a leading French Catholic, Pierre-Daniel Huet, attended the synagogue with Menasseh. All of this would suggest a fairly friendly ambiance in which younger members would not be expected to avoid interchanges with people of other religious beliefs.

Another major reason that has been given as to what may have been involved in the Spinoza case is Spinoza's adherence to Cartesianism. From 1637, René Descartes's new philosophy had appeared in publications in the Netherlands. Cartesianism became a popular point of view during the 1640s and 1650s and led to many social outbursts, such as the major dispute about a professor of medicine at Utrecht adhering to Cartesian principles in the early 1640s. At one point, the Dutch government tried to forbid the discussion of Cartesianism in public cafés because of the violence that ensued.[44] Yet, no matter how much of a public menace the discussion of Cartesianism in the Netherlands may have been at the time, there is no evidence whatsoever that this had any effect within the Jewish community.

Spinoza first published a piece about Cartesianism in 1666, a textbook entitled *Principles of René Descartes's Philosophy*, ten years after his excommunication. There is no evidence that Cartesianism was a problem within the Jewish community at the time of Spinoza's excommunication. The Jewish intellectuals who had studied in Spanish and French universities make no mention of Cartesianism and none of them seems to have been attracted to the Cartesian influences in the Netherlands.

A further point that needs to be considered is that the leaders of the Spanish Portuguese synagogue seem to have had little interest in major theological or religious topics. In an important study entitled "Why was Baruch de Spinoza Excommunicated?" Asa Kasher and Shlomo Biderman made an effort to find out if any of the Amsterdam rabbis or leaders were known for any theological points.[45] There is a vast computer index of rabbinical *Responsa* located at the Museum of the Diaspora at Tel Aviv University. The only rabbi from the Amsterdam synagogue of the seventeenth century who appears in the database is Menasseh ben Israel, not for any theological view but for certain word usages. The word usages are not surprising in that Menasseh worked on the Hebrew grammar and lexicon of the Christian Hebraist, J. Buxtorf. Rabbis from other Jewish centers in Europe have many entries. This also reflects the fact that other rabbis did not ask the opinion of Amsterdam religious leaders about matters concerning Judaism, presumably because they did not think they had important views.

If the rabbis of the Amsterdam synagogue were not impressive religious figures, the *parnassim* were less so. They were essentially business and community leaders, presumably chosen because of their wealth and because of what they could do for the community. Research concerning the leaders of the Amsterdam synagogue by Daniel Swetschinski and Miriam Bodian show their interests to be primarily commercial and economic with little religious import. A study by one of the early members of the Amsterdam stock exchange indicates the same point of view.[46] From what we know of the lay leadership of the Amsterdam community there does not seem to be any source of hostility to radical ideas. It may well be that it was the way Spinoza presented the ideas rather than the ideas themselves that brought about such a strong reaction.

A further possibility to explain what happened has recently been put forth by Odette Vlessing, a scholar of the Amsterdam fiscal records of the time. It has been known for quite a while that Spinoza was having difficulties with the civil fiscal authorities in Amsterdam in the 1650s. Spinoza's father was a businessman engaged in a great deal of commerce in fruits, wine, and vegetables from southern Europe and North Africa into northern Europe. He seems to have been quite successful until the 1650s when some ships carrying his cargo were seized by the English during the Anglo-Dutch war and others were looted by pirates. Spinoza's mother had died in 1638; his father remarried, and withheld what would have been young Spinoza's inheritance from his mother in an effort to save his own business. His business declined however and, a year and a half after the death of his second wife, Michael Espinoza died in 1654 leaving many debts behind him. Spinoza sought legal protection as an orphan for his mother's estate and legal protection as a minor to avoid any consequences of his father's bankruptcy. Records in 1656 show the case getting more and more difficult. Spinoza hired a lawyer, who incidentally was the lawyer for Titus Rembrandt, the son of the great artist, who had similar problems concerning the house in the Jewish quarter that his father had transferred to him before declaring bankruptcy. Vlessing suggests that Spinoza was on the verge of making the Jewish community a party to his financial problems and that they wanted very much to separate themselves from his tax problems. In order to avoid any scandal in the Jewish community and to avoid being held accountable for Spinoza's debts, the *parnassim* had only one option – to declare Spinoza a heretic and excommunicate him.[47]

Jonathan Israel has offered a somewhat different scenario in which Spinoza wanted to be excommunicated so that he would no longer be tied down by the Jewish communities' problems and wishes. According to Israel, Spinoza had become so radical that he saw that his future lay in getting as far away from his ancestral roots as possible. To do this, he would have to make the community do the work of pushing him aside. But to make it stick legally Israel shows that the community tried over and over again to find a formulation by which Spinoza could be his own man and still be a member of the community. Spinoza rejected all these formulations and, in Israel's picture, became more and more hostile each time until the community felt they had had enough. They finally had to bring the matter to an end, hence the very strongly worded excommunication.[48]

Another theory that is being strongly promulgated at the present time is that offered by Steven Nadler in his biography of Spinoza. He contends that what led to the excommunication was Spinoza's view denying the immortality of the soul. Nadler points out, as discussed in the previous chapter, that this had been a divisive issue back in 1640 when Uriel da Costa was excommunicated. Nadler has to work very hard to find any indication that Spinoza had any view about the immortality of the soul before his excommunication and does this only by reading backwards from later statements and works. Nadler assumes that all Sephardic communities at the time would have had a similar outlook, but, as Yosef Kaplan and I have argued, the Western Sephardic communities – Amsterdam, Hamburg, and London, for example – were less inclined to doctrines and rituals.[49] They were mainly made up of people who had been raised as Christians and who enjoyed being Jewish as long as it did not make their lives difficult. Most of them had little knowledge of Sephardic religious traditions on most matters. Their main concern seems to have been to keep their community flourishing within the liberal societies in which it was allowed to function.

We can only hope that more material will become available in the future that will help in assessing Spinoza's case. It was thought for a long time that the Sephardic community in Amsterdam was secretly hiding material about Spinoza and this was one reason for their reluctance to allow scholars into their archives. However, after the archives of Ets Haim became part of public materials and many scholars started working there it turned out that there was nothing about Spinoza. What they were hiding was material about how many members of the congregation in the 1660s and 1670s were followers of Sabbatai Zevi, the alleged Jewish messiah of the seventeenth century.

Other sources of information about Spinoza's excommunication are the early biographies of the philosopher. In Bayle and Lucas there is no description of any ceremony involved in the excommunication. Bayle describes it as an on-going argument that finally ended with the synagogue excommunicating Spinoza and Spinoza leaving. There is no sense of drama or a point at which it all came to a head. The same is the case in Lucas. In both, Spinoza is portrayed as leaving Amsterdam because somebody tried to kill him with a knife, either outside the synagogue or a theater depending on the source, rather than any theological differences with the community.

Bayle, using material from a biography written around 1680 that was in manuscript and seems to have disappeared, tried to find out more details but could not gain any more information. In his biography of Spinoza, Bayle makes the excommunication into a series of disagreements between Spinoza and the religious authorities, finally ending up with a mutual decision to break off further discussions. Spinoza did this by moving away and the community by issuing a *pro forma* excommunication. In no way is Spinoza portrayed as a victim of religious persecution and, similarly, Spinoza himself never said anything that would indicate he regarded himself in such a manner.

Bayle's friend Jacques Basnage tried to find somebody who could tell him what happened at the excommunication. Yet, nobody had any information. Basnage asked an elderly rabbi, probably Isaac Aboab, who just told him that Spinoza plagiarized from the kabbalists in the Jewish community and tried to make himself appear original by using Descartes's terminology.[50]

Colerus also tried to find an eyewitness but could find nobody who was present. Thus, Colerus researched what a Jewish excommunication was supposed to be like according to ancient Jewish laws. He took the account, which appears in John Selden's *Historie of Tithes*, which describes the monumentally solemn excommunication affair with processions, chants, and black candles held upside down.[51] This is presented without claiming this is what happened in Spinoza's case. In fact, probably none of this occurred in Spinoza's case. Nevertheless, because of popular accounts such as that of Colerus, the history of Spinoza as a martyr and victim was created.

It is important to note that nobody at the time knew the actual statement of condemnation of Spinoza. This statement is first published by Jacob Freudenthal in his book *Spinoza: Sein Leben und seine Lehre*.[52] The text of the excommunication, which now seems so ferocious and barbaric, was supposedly sitting in a closet from the time in 1656 when Spinoza was excommunicated until it emerged in the 1840s. It has now become the best-known thing about Spinoza and is repeated by Bertrand Russell among others as evidence of how intolerant and ruthless religious groups can be.

If my reconstruction is correct, people at the time would not have known about the severity of the charges. They probably would have known what appears in Bayle's account – that there was a period of charges and counter-charges and that there were attempts on the part of the community and its officials to keep Spinoza in the fold and to keep him from being disruptive. They probably would have known that he had rebuffed offers to defuse his case by giving him minimal participation in the community's affairs, providing he would not make trouble. Yet, Spinoza at some point decided it was not worth staying within the fold and moved outside the community. Likewise, the community at some point decided it was not worth trying to keep Spinoza and closed the case by conducting a quiet, non-public excommunication.

At the time of the expulsion Spinoza was living with the Collegiants, outside the Jewish community, and was thus involved with radical and millenarian Protestants who were *sans église*. The expulsion simply formalized a state of affairs that already existed. So, Spinoza went off, not as a victim or a pariah but as an independent Portuguese person living in Amsterdam. In so doing, he became one of the first people to live outside of any religious affiliation.

Outside the synagogue: millenarian Protestantism and radical politics

As we saw in the previous chapter, Spinoza had begun his intellectual journey outside the Jewish community some time prior to his excommunication. What role his teacher Menasseh ben Israel played in putting Spinoza in contact with radical or millenarian Protestants is hard to discern. Menasseh was one of the main teachers in the community's educational service. He was second in importance among the rabbis and was a renowned preacher. He was also the leading printer and publisher in Hebrew language books and materials relating to Judaism. In these capacities and in explaining Jewish views to a broader audience, Menasseh came in contact with many Protestant figures in the Netherlands and became acquainted with some of the leading English millenarian thinkers who passed through the Netherlands.

A major theme that pervaded discussions around the synagogue was that of whether the messianic age was really imminent. Many Christian millenarians in the Netherlands and England had strong expectations that the messianic era would begin in 1655–6. Calculations made from the Book of Daniel and the Book of Revelation led various scholars to center on these dates.

Chapter Four

Menasseh ben Israel's trip to England in 1655–7 to try to elicit the readmission of the Jews was obviously more than just one man's fantasy. On the contrary, it was a major public indication that the pre-messianic events were being discussed at the highest levels of English parliamentary government. This would also have enormous implications for the Jewish community of Amsterdam. A sign of the interdenominational character of these events is that the leader of the Dutch Collegiants, Adam Boreel, was present at some of the governmental meetings in England concerning Menasseh's petition to Cromwell. In fact, he entertained Menasseh at a dinner in London during this period. Boreel was also in Amsterdam a few months before and a few months after.

Could Spinoza have been unaware of the messianic excitement that was taking place within the Jewish community and within the community of the radical Protestants? It is hard to believe that Spinoza was oblivious both to the millenarian excitement about the possible beginning of the end of human history and the Sephardic hope that they would have a new homeland. It seems certain that both of these momentous scenarios were discussed inside and outside the synagogue.

Spinoza, now living with the Collegiants outside the Jewish community, presumably took part in their spiritual activities. The Collegiants were called *Chrétiens sans église* so Spinoza's contact with them would not involve him having to join a Christian group attached to an organized church.[53] Spinoza was also in close contact with Peter Serrarius, the radical Protestant Amsterdam merchant who was looking for signs that the messiah was about to arrive. Serrarius became Spinoza's contact with the outside world, receiving and sending messages to and from Spinoza to people in other countries. He also seems to have played some role in Spinoza's early publications. Serrarius published quite a few pamphlets about impending millenarian and messianic events. He is thought to be the author of one pamphlet about a ship with silver sails coming into the harbor at Aberdeen with signs saying "We Are the Lost Tribes of Israel." He checked and rechecked his suspicions about divine signs with the rabbis in the Jewish community and became extremely involved with the Sabbatian messianic movement.[54]

One would not realize Serrarius's role in Spinoza's affairs from the surviving material of Spinoza's correspondence. He is only mentioned once. However, when the correspondence of Sir Henry Oldenburg was published in the 1980s, Serrarius is shown to have played a significant role as patron and guardian of Spinoza's relations with people outside the Netherlands. Serrarius himself was a Scot and closely involved with such people as the millenarian John Dury. He and Dury attended the same Walloon seminary in Leiden and they shared contacts with the group that Charles Webster has called the "Spiritual Brotherhood," intellectuals who sought to find religious meaning in the events of the time.[55]

Spinoza also became more involved with the Quakers immediately after the excommunication. The leader of the Quakers at the time, Margaret Fell, had written two pamphlets urging the Jews to convert. One of these she addressed specifically to Menasseh ben Israel when he was in England. She hoped that the pamphlets could be translated into Hebrew so that Jews could actually read them. The translation chore was entrusted to Samuel Fisher, the only one of the early Quakers who had had a university education. Fisher had made scant progress in the translation task when he moved to the Netherlands with the Quaker refugees. There, he began working with a Jew who knew Portuguese and Dutch as well as Hebrew and the two of them proceeded to translate one of the pamphlets. There is reason to suspect that the Jewish translator was Spinoza, though this cannot be completely established on present evidence. Fisher left Amsterdam in 1658 on a quixotic mission to convert the pope and the sultan. All we know is that he returned quite rich and that on setting foot in England once again he published a huge volume *The Rustick Alarm to the Rabbies* in 1660. This book of more than seven hundred pages raises almost all of the points that Spinoza would later present in his criticism of the Bible. Fisher's work is in English, while Spinoza's work, the *Tractatus Theologico-Politicus*, published in 1670, is in Latin. It does seem most unusual that the only two people in Europe at the time to see the many philological, historical, and cultural points that would cast doubt on whether we now possess an accurate and authentic copy of the Word of God were Samuel Fisher and Baruch de Spinoza, who had probably known each other around 1656–7. Both of them had built on the earlier biblical criticism of Thomas Hobbes and Isaac La Peyrère and developed their critical points into a full-fledged skepticism about the existence of a veridical text of God's message to mankind.[56]

Spinoza also collaborated on another pamphlet in 1661 and it is in this work that the metaphysical foundation of moral certainty that Spinoza presents in his *Tractatus* can be discerned. Pieter Balling, a member of the Amsterdam philosophical group that was supporting Spinoza financially, was chosen to visit Spinoza to ask for his help in writing this philosophical pamphlet, because he was fluent in Spanish and could talk to Spinoza more easily. The pamphlet justifying a Quaker-like theology was entitled *Light on a Candlestick*. The terminology of the pamphlet seems to come from Spinoza's formulation of the bases of higher knowledge. The pamphlet was published in 1662 and since then has appeared over and over again as an appendix to William Sewell's *History of the Quakers*.[57]

In 1659, Spinoza, along with fellow heretic Juan de Prado, attended a philosophical theological discussion group in Amsterdam. This group was formed by Spanish-speaking members of the Jewish community who met in the home of a medical doctor. Two reports of one such meeting have come down to us in the papers of the Spanish Inquisition. The Inquisition wanted to keep track of the activities of Spaniards who had moved to the Netherlands and asked travelers to report on any interesting activities they came across. A Spanish sea captain and a monk independently reported on the same meeting at which rabbis and Jewish laymen were present as well as Spinoza and Prado. The latter two explained that they had been excommunicated and that they did not believe very much, only "that God exists but only philosophically" and that the soul is mortal and dies with the body. No further expansion or detail as to what this meant for them was given. This is the only statement we have of Spinoza's views while he was still in Amsterdam. In light of what he was to write in the next several years, it is clear that he was moving in a more metaphysical direction. It is worth noting that in spite of the severe demands in the excommunication statement that no Jew communicate with Spinoza or be in his presence, the accounts of the sea captain and the monk indicate that both rabbis and laypersons were at this meeting and that nothing was said about the fact that they should not have contact with the miscreant Spinoza. Considering the fact that Spinoza's excommunication was not made public until the nineteenth century and that nobody seems to mention the case, it therefore seems possible that the excommunication was not a public ceremonial event but one held *in camera*. Thus, the Jews present at this 1659 meeting may not have known that they were not supposed to be anywhere near Spinoza, even though the excommunication order specifies how many cubits they were to allow between themselves and the heretic.[58]

There has been a flurry of recent interest in Franciscus Van den Enden's political influence on Spinoza. Van den Enden was not merely a Latin teacher but also a radical thinker in politics and religion. A few years ago, two of his writings were discovered in which some of the same phrases that Spinoza made famous appear, specifically concerning the identity of God and Nature. Since the works date from 1661, they could just as easily be the result of Spinoza telling his teacher about his theory rather than vice versa. In addition, there is nothing in Van den Enden's writings that indicate he had any opinions about the Bible or

Jewish history, topics that are all important in Spinoza's major work *Tractatus Theologico-Politicus*.[59]

From about 1655 onward, Spinoza was, as we have seen above, involved with a wide variety of radical religious thinkers and with some of those who were bordering on genuine irreligion. We do not have enough information to place where he was in these groups and how much they influenced him or he them. It is unfortunate that when he died his students decided to destroy all his correspondence that was not sufficiently philosophical in their eyes. So we have little or no documentation from Spinoza's side about his contacts. We can only hope that further studies in intellectual history of the period will reveal a bit more about who Spinoza knew, who he talked to, and with whom he exchanged ideas.

Rijnsburg

Spinoza left Amsterdam in 1661 and moved to Rijnsburg, his stated motivation being the attack on him outside the synagogue or theater. After living with another group of Collegiants for a while, he moved to the small cottage that is now displayed as Spinoza's house, where he studied and carried out his craft of lens grinding and specialty optical work for scientists such as Leibniz and Huygens.

Before he left Amsterdam he had become involved with a small group of people interested in philosophy led by a rich merchant Simon de Vries. This group found Spinoza's participation essential to their intellectual enterprise. De Vries offered him a pension that he could receive for the rest of his life if he remained philosophically involved with them. Spinoza felt they were offering him too much money and finally settled for half the original amount, which sufficed to keep him alive in body and soul at a fairly minimal level. It also made it possible for him to visit with them from time to time in Amsterdam or elsewhere.

One of the most important events in Spinoza's intellectual life took place in Rijnsburg shortly after he had moved there. Sir Henry Oldenburg, who was to become secretary of the Royal Society of England, came to visit him. Oldenburg had either heard about Spinoza from

Peter Serrarius, the publisher Jan Rieuwertsz, or even from Menasseh ben Israel. The latter had met Oldenburg during his visit to England and Oldenburg describes having a lengthy talk with Menasseh at a dinner party in London.

Spinoza was hardly known outside the small circles in which he operated but Oldenburg had no problem finding him. They spent one whole day together and out of this formed a lifetime friendship. They never actually met again in person but over a third of Spinoza's letters are to and from Oldenburg and continue up to the very end of Spinoza's life. Oldenburg immediately put Spinoza in contact with Oldenburg's patron, Sir Robert Boyle, and Spinoza was shortly discussing metaphysics and chemistry with the great scientist. Oldenburg was so impressed with Spinoza's intellectual capacity that for the next couple of years he kept offering to help arrange for the publication of any of Spinoza's work. There seems little indication at the outset that Oldenburg realized or cared about the immense gulf that separated their ideas. It is only much later on, after Oldenburg had read Spinoza's *Tractatus*, that he saw Spinoza as an opponent of any supernatural formulation of Christianity.[60]

Oldenburg was also more interested in messianic events than Spinoza appeared to be. In December 1665, Oldenburg wrote to Spinoza as follows:

> But I turn to politics. Here there is a wide-spread rumour that the Israelites, who have been dispersed for more than two thousand years, are to return to their homeland. Few hereabouts believe it, but many wish it. Do let your friend know what you hear about this matter, and what you think. For my part, I cannot put any faith in this news, as long as it is not reported by trustworthy men from the city of Constantinople, which is most of all concerned in this matter. I am anxious to know what the Jews of Amsterdam have heard about it, and how they are affected by so momentous an announcement, which, if true, is likely to bring about a world crisis.[61]

This is no doubt a question raised because of the tumult that was occurring in the Ottoman Empire when a religious figure from Smyrna, Sabbatai Zevi, declared he was the long-awaited Jewish messiah in 1665. Acting his part, Sabbatai revised Jewish law, some of the prayers and holidays, and appointed ten kings of the world to rule with him. This caused a tremendous stir not only in Turkey but also all over the Jewish world. News of it got to Europe and Jewish communities in London and Amsterdam were very much affected. In fact, Amsterdam became one of the most active centers of Sabbatianism. One of the first letters Sabbatai Zevi wrote to announce his arrival as messiah and his new status in the universe was sent to the Amsterdam Jewish community and is still among its treasures.[62]

Oldenburg probably heard of the letter from some of his contacts in London and asked his friend Spinoza for some information about the matter, as the above quotation indicates. Oldenburg was very excited and interested in this development in Jewish history. Yet, there is no sign that Spinoza sent Oldenburg a response.[63] Oldenburg tried to gain further information about Sabbatianism from other people he knew in the Netherlands, including Peter Serrarius. The Christian millenarian merchant was in constant contact with the Amsterdam synagogue about possible signs that the Jewish messiah was arriving or the Jews were about to convert. Serrarius, in fact, saw the letter Sabbatai Zevi sent to the Amsterdam community and made a copy of it for his friend John Dury, who was then in Germany and Switzerland, trying to reunite the Protestant churches of Europe. Serrarius received this letter to Spinoza from Oldenburg and sent it on to him. Serrarius wrote his own answer, which Oldenburg apparently never received, in which he revealed how convinced he was that Sabbatai Zevi was the king of the Jews:

> As for the Jews their hope revives more and more. Those of Vienna having sent an Expres to Adrianopolis, do writ, that their Man doth affirm, to have spoken with Sabithai Sebi and found him, not turned Turck, but a Jew as ever in the same hope and expectation as before. Yea, from Smyrna by way of marcelles we have, that at

47

Constantinople the Jews return to their fasting and praying as before: and so doe some here likewise. It appears both in regard of Christians & of Jews, that Gods Worcks ever were a riddle to flesh and bloud, and a stumbling-block to worldly minds.[64]

Serrarius apparently even became a believer that Sabbatai Zevi was the expected messiah. He worked out a theory that the Sabbatian appearance was a stage in the Jews finding their way to a higher Judaism and finally to Christianity. Serrarius died on his way to meet Sabbatai.

Newspapers carried accounts about the Sabbatian movement in almost every issue during the years 1665–6. Given the excitement in Amsterdam and in England about Sabbatai Zevi it is hard to believe that Spinoza knew nothing about this. We know that the Amsterdam stock exchange went berserk when the news about Sabbatai Zevi's messianic pronouncement appeared. People, Jews and non-Jews alike, did not know whether to buy or sell, and whether the world was really being transformed. Spinoza's correspondence indicates that he kept on the news of events in England and Europe in general. Certainly, Spinoza cannot have been unaware of the fuss concerning Sabbatai Zevi or of the fact that the rules of orthodox Judaism had been set aside by a considerable number of people. It is therefore hard to believe that he did not know, or care about, a development that was causing so much excitement all over Europe and even America where the New England preachers were trying to find out if the expected messiah had actually turned up.

The matter became more exciting and controversial when Sabbatai Zevi, in 1666, converted to Islam after being arrested by the Sultan. The Jewish world was in turmoil. The effects of Sabbatai's conversion were extremely disruptive in the Amsterdam Jewish community. At the outset, in 1665–6, almost all the members of the synagogue became followers. After the conversion, many were in despair and went back to normative Judaism, while some evolved theologies that still portrayed

Sabbatai Zevi as the messiah whose conversion was part of the messianic drama. They believed that he would explain all of this when he resumed his messianic career in glory. We know now that the effects of all this in Amsterdam were traumatic for the Jewish community *and* for many of those in the Christian community who were concerned about possible relations between Jewish messianism and Christian millenarianism at the time. This, of course, included many people whom Spinoza knew. One wonders why, with Spinoza's critical attitude toward Judaism, he did not say a word about the farcical results of a Jewish messiah turned Muslim. It is really surprising that Spinoza did not say a word on this subject or, if he did, that his student heirs destroyed the documents.

From the time he met Oldenburg, Spinoza was apparently working on several intellectual projects, possibly trying to determine the best way to present his philosophy. One of these was the unfinished treatise on the improvement of the intellect, *Tractatus de intellectus emendatione* (Treatise on the Emendation of the Intellect), and the other a short treatise in Dutch, *Korte verhandeling van God, de mensch en deszelfs welstand* (A Short Treatise on God, Man and His Well-Being). The latter is the only work that Spinoza wrote in Dutch.

Spinoza was also drafting a way of studying and evaluating Descartes's philosophy, concerned with the development of certain features of Cartesianism. In the early 1660s he had been giving lessons to advanced students on philosophy and apparently introduced them to Cartesianism as a way of getting to his own intellectual world that he was developing. In a work that he had not planned to publish, *René Descartes's Principles of Philosophy*, Spinoza indicated problems with Descartes's formulations (although he left the clarification of this for his major work, the *Ethics*). This probably started as a teaching manual for students who came to study with him. His Amsterdam friends took it to the printer and it became the first philosophical publication of Spinoza.

One can see Spinoza's own views emerging in certain parts of the *Principles* but he did not openly present them at this early date. Spinoza was impressed by the possibilities of basing philosophical exposition on the geometrical method. Although philosophers from ancient times to the present have extolled rational exposition as the way to present their cases and may have seen the method used in Euclid's geometry as ideal, few have ever tried to emulate the purely rational procedures of mathematicians. If one had axioms that were beyond question and logical methods of proceeding, then everything developed from this should be beyond question.

Later, Spinoza gave an indication of the advantage of this in his brief discussion of Euclid in the *Tractatus* where he says:

> Euclid, whose writings are concerned only with things exceedingly simple and perfectly intelligible, is easily made clear by anyone in any language; for in order to grasp his thought and to be assured of his true meaning there is no need to have a thorough knowledge of the language in which he wrote. A superficial and rudimentary knowledge in enough. Nor need we enquire into the author's life, pursuits and character, the language in which he wrote, and for whom and when, nor what happened to his book, nor its different readings, nor how it came to be accepted and by what council. And what we here say of Euclid can be said of all who have written on matters which of their very nature are capable of intellectual apprehension.[65]

Of course, Spinoza turned out to be wrong about this. Those who study the history of mathematics have traced developments that led to Euclid's presentation and the contexts in which certain ideas and theorems became important. The development of alternative geometrical systems in the nineteenth and twentieth centuries has also presented different perspectives for viewing earlier Greek mathematics. Spinoza may have wanted to avoid contextualism by following the geometrical method but he could not take either his work or Euclid's out of history. Hence, a historian such as G. W. Heath in *The History of Mathematics* could explain the development of Euclidean writings in terms of various factors in Greek history and many historians have been explaining Spinoza's geometrical presentation in its historical context.

In spite of the above advantage, one rarely finds attempts to develop a geometrically based philosophy. In antiquity there is just one example, that of the Neoplatonist Proclus (410–485), who wrote *Elements of Theology* and presented Neoplatonic theology in an axiomatic deductive system. It is extremely cumbersome and did not attract any followers in methodology.

Closer to Spinoza's time, the question of whether philosophy could be presented in geometrical form was raised in Father Marin Mersenne's *Second Set of Objections* to Descartes's philosophy. Mersenne, who had been a student at the same Jesuit college that Descartes had attended, was also a teacher of mathematics. He thought that Descartes could make his new philosophy more attractive if he could present it in a geometrical manner. Descartes tried to do so in an appendix to his reply to Mersenne in which almost all the philosophy becomes part of the axiom system. The deductive part consists of four theorems, three of which say God exists and the fourth that there is an essential difference between Mind and Matter.

Spinoza worked out the geometrical system in more detail, deriving one portion from another. He was concerned to show the logical relationship from start to finish. In this, he both follows Descartes and begins to indicate where he differs from him. For Spinoza, there is no necessity to start philosophizing from a rejection of scepticism nor is there any reason to present it as part of one's own autobiography as in Descartes's *Discourse on Method,* or as reflections of one's own thoughts, as in Descartes's *Meditations on First Philosophy.* Instead, one should be able to move logically step by step. The central concept that makes this possible is that of substance, or God. Spinoza says in many places in his writings that there is no need to consider any skeptical problems if one is aware of the idea of God. This becomes the evidence of itself and explains everything else.

At the outset of the *Principles*, Spinoza omitted Cartesian doubt as one of Descartes's means of searching for truth. Spinoza said the effect of Descartes's method was that "he undertook to reduce everything to doubt, not like a sceptic, who apprehends no other end than doubt itself, but in order to free his mind from all prejudice."[66] Descartes hoped to discover the firm and unshakable foundations of science, which could not escape him if he followed the method. "For the true principles of knowledge should be so clear and certain as to need no proof, should be placed beyond all hazard of doubt, and should be such that nothing could be proved without them."[67] It is the existence of such principles (and the intellectual catastrophe if there is none) to which Spinoza will appeal in his skirmishes with the skeptics. What removes all the Cartesian doubts is that one knows "that the faculty of distinguishing true and false had not been given to him by a supremely good and truthful God in order that he might be deceived."[68] In discussing this, Spinoza made his fundamental basis of certainty clear.

> For, as is obvious from everything that has already been said, the pivot of the entire matter is this, that we can form a concept of God which so disposes us that we cannot with equal ease suppose that he is deceiver as that he is not, but which compels us to affirm that he is entirely truthful. But when we have formed such an idea, the reason for doubting mathematical truths is removed. For then whenever we turn our minds in order to doubt any one of these things, just as in the case of our existence, we find nothing to prevent our concluding that it is entirely certain.[69]

Spinoza went on to present Descartes's theory and, in the course of the presentation, made the centrality of the idea of God obvious. He claimed that there was no point in arguing with people who deny they have the idea. That would be like trying to teach a blind man colors. "But unless we are willing to regard these people as a new kind of animal, midway between men and brutes, we should pay little attention to their words."[70] The centrality is shown again as Spinoza presents the propositions that make up Descartes' philosophy. The criterion of truth, "Whatever we clearly and distinctly perceive is true", follows after "God is utterly truthful and is not at all a deceiver."[71] Descartes had used the criterion to prove that God was not a deceiver. In Spinoza's world the idea of God precludes deception and guarantees that clear and distinct ideas are true.

In Spinoza's own attempt to develop his philosophy methodologically in the *Treatise on the Improvement of the Understanding*, after he had developed his method for discovering certain truth, he stopped to consider the possibility that there yet remains some skeptic who may have doubts of our primary truth and of all the deductions we make. Taking such truth as our standard, he must either be arguing in bad faith, or we must confess that there are men in complete mental blindness, either innate or due to misconceptions – that is, to some external influence. The classification of the skeptic as mentally blind had already occurred in the *Principles*. One wonders what evidence Spinoza could give besides appealing to how clear and certain various truths were to him.

Spinoza was obviously perplexed by his supposed skeptic. He went on to say that the skeptic could not affirm or doubt anything; he cannot even say that he knows nothing – in fact, he "ought to remain dumb for fear of haply supposing something which should smack of truth."[72] If these skeptics "deny, grant or gainsay, they know not that they deny, grant or gainsay, so that they ought to be regarded as automata, utterly devoid of intelligence."[73]

In all of Spinoza's comments so far, there is basically an *ad hominem* argument about the mentality and character of the skeptic or doubter. Spinoza has yet to come to grips with the skeptic's arguments, regardless of whether the skeptic is in a position to affirm or deny them. In the *Improvement of the Understanding*, Spinoza made clear what is at issue: "Hence we cannot cast doubt on true ideas by the supposition that there is a deceitful Deity, who leads us astray even in what is most certain. We can only hold such an hypothesis so long as we have no clear and distinct idea."[74] When we reflect on the idea of God, we know that he can be no deceiver with the same certitude as we know that the sum of the angles of a triangle equals two right angles. Spinoza, also in the *Improvement of the Understanding*, brushed aside the possibility that the search for truth would lead to an infinite regress of seeking a method, and seeking a method for finding the method, and so on. Spinoza insisted that

> in order to discover the truth, there is no need of another method to discover such method; nor of a third method for discovering the second, and so on to infinity. By such proceedings, we should never arrive at any knowledge of the truth, or indeed, at any knowledge at all … the intellect, by its native strength, makes for itself intellectual instruments, whereby it acquires strength for performing other intellectual operations, and from these operations get, again, fresh instruments, or the power of pushing its investigations further, and thus gradually proceeds till it reaches the summit of wisdom.[75]

Spinoza makes the mathematical proposition of the sum of the angles of a triangle co-equal to the metaphysical one in that the certainty is self-evident in both cases. In this way, he sidesteps or avoids the whole encounter with skepticism that plagued Descartes, possibly because he never lived through the skeptical crisis that produced Descartes's philosophy. Instead, Spinoza's outlook is shaped by the certainty of mathematical concepts and their explanatory power.

Spinoza differs from Descartes on the all-important subject of the nature of substance. Descartes's world consisted of three substances – God, Mind, and Matter – in which God is the cause of the other two. Spinoza, as we shall see, makes the logic of substantial philosophy the measure of understanding anything. Descartes said that he used the term "substance" equivocally; it had one meaning when talking of God and a different one when speaking about the two explanatory categories, Mind and Matter. There was much discussion among Cartesians in the period from 1650 to 1670 concerning the problem of how two completely separate substances, Mind and Matter, having no attribute in common, could interact. Descartes maintained that the interaction takes place in the pineal gland at the base of the brain, though he did not satisfy people about how this mysterious interaction took place. Even while Descartes was still alive he was pressed to give some explanation and he told Princess Elizabeth of Bohemia that this is one of those matters that one understands best by thinking about it least. He also exclaimed that peasants know about Mind/Body interaction without thinking, so why do philosophers have such troubles? In the decade after Descartes's death in 1650, a range of explanations were developed, culminating in the occasionalist philosophy of Geulincx and Malebranche. Spinoza, by insisting on the primary notion of substance, would develop a philosophy in which this Mind/Body interaction problem would have an easy, if not really believable, solution.

As mentioned earlier, one obvious advantage of the geometrical method is that no contact has to be established between the author and the reader. Descartes, in contrast, kept trying to figure out the best form in which to present his theory. He first wrote it out as a set of rules for improving human reasoning. Next, he decided to present it after an autobiographical explanation as to how he came to the theory. Then, the third time, he presented it as the meditations, or musings, about what human beings could know with any certainty. And finally, in its most didactic form, it was presented as principles of human knowledge. Descartes did furnish introductions and dedications. As the introduction to the *Meditations* shows he was very concerned about how intellectual authorities would treat his views. His letter to the Jesuits and his statement to the doctors of theology at the Sorbonne are attempts to establish a good relationship with some of his most important potential readers. Descartes has to explain that there is nothing irreligious in his work, that he is not in any way differing from the Roman Catholic Church, and that he has no intention of dealing with theology. Spinoza, on the other hand, did not feel any of this was necessary.

By the time the *Principles* appeared Spinoza had moved on from Rijnsburg, in 1663, to the outskirts of The Hague. His circle of acquaintances grew much larger and included professors, medical doctors, political figures, and people in the cultural world. Spinoza gradually got to know various people interested in scientific research in the Netherlands. His own achievements as a lens-grinder and theoretician of optics became known to figures like Christian Huygens, among others. Huygens and Spinoza were in contact in the mid-1660s, exchanged ideas, and met sometimes during the next years. Huygens was impressed by Spinoza's achievements with lenses but had his doubts about Spinoza as a scientific theoretician. Huygens, then the most prominent scientist in the Netherlands, was basically an empiricist and dubious about theoretical claims by Descartes. So he and Spinoza parted on various points then in dispute. It is also interesting to note that Huygens in his letters to his brother refers to Spinoza as "the Jew," "the Israelite," and so on, and Huygens, who was from the upper strata of Dutch society, found Spinoza a bit too far below him. However, it was through Huygens that Spinoza came into contact with other Dutch scientists of the period.[76]

Spinoza also became involved with some of the avant-garde critics of organized religion including Dr. Lodewijk Meyer and Adriaan Koerbagh. This led to his most daring publication, the *Tractatus Theologico-Politicus*.

Chapter Six

The *Tractatus Theologico-Politicus*: religion and political society

In the late 1660s Spinoza wrote his *Tractatus Theologico-Politicus* defending complete freedom of speech, thought, and belief. This work was to make him famous and infamous not only in the Netherlands but also in Europe in general. Spinoza's political thought needs to be seen in light of what was going on at the time and especially in light of the travails of Dutch liberalism. There was an ongoing discussion and controversy over who was really in charge of the newly liberated territory. During the seventeenth century, the provinces of Holland tried various forms of government, finally ending up with a very limited monarchy.

Spinoza tried in various early writings to find the best way to present his overall philosophy. He was concerned with the problem that Descartes had raised at the outset of his *Discourse on Method*, namely, whether the way in which a truth-seeker lived affected whether he would be able to find the truth. Descartes sought a provisionary morality that committed him to the least number of principles. Spinoza went further in contending that his minimalist lifestyle was the best way to keep from closing off possible solutions to man's quest for the highest good. Other lifestyles, such as seeking fame or fortune, could distract one from finding the prize; supposedly, the minimalist lifestyle obligated one to so little that there was less danger of excluding higher goods.

In the relatively pluralist and free society of the Netherlands, with its abundance of religious groups, Spinoza was able to examine their different claims and practices. The multiplicity of religious perspectives also seemed to involve the seeds of perpetual strife as one group vied with another over which one had the better or truer vision of the world. This friction, if not controlled, could lead to civil war and the dissolution of the society. Spinoza argued that most people were baffled by what went on around them and readily accepted superstitious answers. As long as they are in such a state of credulity, he contended, they could be easily duped and led into conflict with other people. With the ongoing struggle over who would control the Netherlands, Spinoza was concerned about the political situation, fearing the kind of civil turmoil that had occurred in England during the period 1640–60, and seems to have gravitated towards those democratic leaders who would keep the state independent of the church. The leading figure in Dutch republicanism of the time was Jan de Witt, the Grand Pensionary, who directed Dutch affairs in the late 1660s and early 1670s. De Witt advocated a relatively tolerant policy towards dissident groups and people. He was also fascinated by the science of the time and was supposed to have been interested in Cartesian mathematics.[77]

Spinoza was probably ruminating about the malevolent features of a religious society from the time he was in difficulties with the synagogue. He also knew about what happened to Isaac La Peyrère for advancing radical religious ideas and the trouble some of his close associates, such as Adriaan Koerbagh, were in for offering daring hypotheses. He saw that a detailed study of religion had great political consequences and that a political society had to come to terms with the religious beliefs of its citizens. Theology and politics were not two subjects to be studied separately but were part of understanding the ongoing world that included recent religious wars, such as the English Civil War and the Thirty Years War. In the preface to the *Tractatus* he wrote,

> Now, seeing that we have the rare happiness of living in a republic, where everyone's judgment is free and unshackled, where each may worship God as his conscience dictates, and where freedom is esteemed before all things dear and precious, I have believed that I should be undertaking no ungrateful or unprofitable task, in demonstrating that not only can such freedom be granted without prejudice to the public peace, but also, that without such freedom, piety cannot flourish nor the public peace be secure.[78]

For Spinoza, a beginning stage in understanding what religion and theology are about is the analysis of the special knowledge that is contained in religious outlooks. Spinoza does this chiefly by looking at the Bible, both what it says and what is said about it, and the prophetic knowledge that the Bible is supposed to tell us about, that is, knowledge that people called prophets have. But what can this be? Spinoza's idea of true knowledge would be either mathematical or empirical scientific knowledge. The prophets, however, do not offer us any mathematical truths that could not be gained independently of Scripture. Neither do they offer us any empirical scientific information that requires a religious context. Thus, Spinoza contends, they are not offering knowledge claims but rather statements of their heightened imaginations.

In a move that was to be most revolutionary, Spinoza contended that the religion of Scripture should be understood in terms of its context. Except for a few hardy souls it had been assumed that Scripture is divine history. Spinoza, however, moved it into human history. What one is dealing with is not a description of God's intervention in human affairs but one of many case histories of people employing religion for human purposes in human affairs. La Peyrère had limited Scripture to being only about Jewish history, but Jewish history was still an essential portion of divine history and contained its culmination with the soon-to-be-expected arrival of the Jewish messiah. Spinoza, in contrast, understood the scriptural world as a description of how at a certain point in human affairs a society was established in which religious symbols were made all-important for the functioning of that society. The Hebrew commonwealth was, in Spinoza's account, established by Moses in a completely human state of affairs. The Israelites had escaped from Egypt and in so doing were then in a state of nature. They were no longer subject to Egyptian law or any other law. Moses made them into a new community by proscribing laws for them and getting them to accept the laws as divine ordinances. Otherwise they would have fallen into a state of anarchy with no person or persons in charge and everyone fighting each other. In Spinoza's time there were people questioning whether Moses, Jesus or Mohammed actually had divine roles or were basically political activists taking over societies. From 1650 onward, the theses of the underground work *Traité des Trois Imposteurs, ou l'Esprit de M. Spinosa* (The Three Imposters, or the Life of Spinoza) were being discussed, the three imposters being Moses, Jesus, and Mohammed. Sir Henry Oldenburg wrote to the Collegiant leader Adam Boreel in 1656 to tell him that such a theory was being debated at Oxford and asked Boreel to help refute it. Spinoza seemed to be following some aspects of the *Three Imposters* thesis in ascribing to Moses the creation of the Hebrew commonwealth. Spinoza was also obliquely challenging those around him who wanted to recreate the Hebrew common-wealth in the Netherlands during the seventeenth century. A popular work called the *Hebrew Commonwealth* by Peter Cunaeus was published and republished. It described both the glories of the original commonwealth and the greater glories it would possess when recreated in modern times.

Spinoza construed the laws and regulations of the Hebrew commonwealth as ceremonial laws. These are human ordi-nances intended to make people aware of the divine importance of what they are doing. As Spinoza described them in Judaism and Christianity, they are efficacious as long as they are relevant to the human situation. However, he claimed that now, long after the events that brought them into existence, the ceremonial laws of Judaism and Christianity are outmoded and unnecessary forms of behavior. The Hebrew commonwealth no longer exists so it does not matter if one follows its ordinances. In Christianity, Spinoza argued that most Christian practices, ceremonial laws that is, are disposed of when they are no longer relevant or easy to perform. He gives the example of the Dutch Christian merchants who went to Japan and promised to leave all their Christian symbols and ceremonies behind them and did so for monetary reasons. Christianity was not relevant in the trade situation. In fact, Spinoza contended that all Christian ceremonial laws were not sacred in and of themselves and thus were "ordained for the preservation of a society" and could be dispensed with or suspended if necessary.[79] In the case of Judaism he was more negative and saw no particular reason to maintain any of the ceremonies. They could be understood historically in terms of when they came to be adopted and what effect this had at a previous time. Putting all this in historical perspective allows one to understand how one religious historical story developed without seeing it as a picture of the history and destiny of all mankind.

In the course of Spinoza's discussion of Jewish ceremonial law, he makes a curious remark that has led to all sorts of commentary. Spinoza argues that Jewish ceremonial law is to be understood in terms of when and why it was instituted and how it functioned. Once the Jewish state no longer existed, the law became irrelevant. Nonetheless, Spinoza said,

> The sign of circumcision is, as I think, so important that I could persuade myself that it alone would preserve the nation for ever. Nay, I would go so far as to believe that if the foundations of their religion have not emasculated their minds they may even, if occasion offers, so changeable are human affairs, raise up their empire afresh, and that God may a second time elect them.[80]

The text does not make clear whether this is some sort of off-color witticism or is intended as a serious possibility of a renewal of Jewish ceremonial law in the future. The Amsterdam Jewish community, in bringing people who had been raised in Christianity back to Judaism, made the circumcision rite the first step that a male had to take to be admitted to the group. This took precedence over celebrating the Sabbath or keeping the dietary rules. There were horrendous stories circulating in the Netherlands of adult *marranos* who circumcised themselves when they returned to the Jewish community or who had it done by somebody else. When he referred to Jewish emasculation, Spinoza may have had the very wealthy Spanish and Portuguese Jews in mind – Jews who displayed themselves in much the same manner as French aristocrats.

It is curious that some commentators often point to this passage as indicating that Spinoza was a proto-Zionist, that he foresaw the possibility of there being a renewed Jewish state. However, there is no indication that Spinoza anticipated any future developments within Jewish history. There is nothing that shows that he was interested in events taking place during his lifetime that might indicate the possibility of new developments in Jewish history. As previously noted, the most important messianic movement, centered on Sabbatai Zevi, was seemingly ignored by Spinoza. If Spinoza had proto-Zionist tendencies one would expect he would have had something to do with messianic Sabbateanism. Otherwise, it is hard to see anything in his remark about the possible regeneration of the Jews that relates to actual Jewish history.

Readers of Spinoza have also been puzzled by his discussions of Christianity. It has been difficult for Jewish commentators to understand Spinoza's laudatory remarks about the role of Jesus, whom he refers to as Christ, and the importance of the Christian message. Some have just written this off as blatant insincerity or as an attempt to curry favor with somebody. However, I think there is a range of possibilities that make more sense of this favorable attitude in terms of debates going on at the time. Some Jews, like his teacher Menasseh ben Israel, sought to combine their religious expectations with those of Christians of the time. Menasseh even seems to have adopted a form of La Peyrère's theory that the king of France would form an alliance with the Jewish messiah and bring about the messianic age. Another rabbi, Nathan Shapira from Jerusalem, turned up in Amsterdam in 1657 trying to raise funds for poor Jews in the Holy Land. He was rebuffed by the synagogue authorities only to find that Protestant millenarians, including Peter Serrarius and John Dury, were very interested in helping him. The Protestants' interest in Shapira's cause arose from discussions they had with him about the supposed differences between Christianity and Judaism. When the rabbi was asked if the messiah had already come he said yes and that, in fact, he comes in every generation but mankind is not good enough to have him stay. Shapira's multiple messianism allowed for the inclusion of Jesus along with all sorts of other figures as instantiations of the messiah. When the rabbi was asked what he thought of the Sermon on the Mount, he said it was the teachings of the most pure and ancient rabbis. Shapira's amalgamation of Judaism and Christianity led Serrarius to say that he could feel Christ within him. The Christians like Dury and Serrarius were so moved by Shapira's apparent philo-Christianity that they started what was for its day a huge fund-raising campaign to help the Jews in the Holy Land. They raised over £4000 in England and the Netherlands. This effort should have been known to Spinoza as well.[81]

On the other hand, some Christians accepted some Jewish practices and beliefs – for example, Jewish dietary laws and the Sabbath as Saturday instead of Sunday – as being completely compatible with their own views. Adam Boreel, the leader of the Collegiants, lived with Rabbi Judah Leon in Amsterdam for four years and they ate the same meals and went to the synagogue together. In general, they saw Judaism as still relevant until the Second Coming that would unify the Jews and Christians.

Spinoza was raised in a world in which such religious inter-action was occurring. In his discussions about Christianity, Spinoza held that the facts recorded in the New Testament of the life of Jesus could be accepted without question. The only item he balked at was the Resurrection, which maintained a gulf between Spinoza's views and those of the majority of Christians, such as his good friend Henry Oldenburg. In his final correspondence with Oldenburg the latter had just read the *Tractatus* and was appalled to see his friend, in his opinion, tearing up Christianity by its roots. Unlike Oldenburg, Spinoza regarded Jesus as completely human but the most perfect human exemplar, the only person who had direct contact with the deity:

> He who firmly believes that God, out of the mercy and grace with which He directs all things, forgives the sins of men, and who feels his love of God kindled thereby, he, I say, does really know Christ according to the Spirit, and Christ is in him.[82]*

As mentioned, Spinoza wrote off Christian ceremonial law in much the way he did Jewish ceremonial law and insisted that what was relevant in the present world was a morality that would keep people from harming each other and make it possible for many people to fulfill their destinies. In these terms, Christianity may have had a stronger moral message for Spinoza that, stripped of any supernatural dimension, he could incorporate into his rational philosophy.

Spinoza contrasted the ceremonial laws of Judaism and Christianity with what he called divine law, which included the laws of nature. Spinoza understood God in terms of natural effects as "the greater our knowledge of natural phenomena, the more perfect is our knowledge of the essence of God (which is the cause of all things)."[83]

---

*This is approximately what Peter Serrarius said about Rabbi Shapira. Spinoza may well have been present at the dinner discussion that took place between Serrarius, Shapira, and a group of Dutch and English millenarians.

Spinoza, in the *Tractatus* and in the unfinished fragment *On the Improvement of the Understanding*, insisted that once one knew the idea of God, skepticism as portrayed by Descartes was not possible. Through this knowledge of God one could understand everything. Hence, some understanding of God could be reached through the study of natural laws.

In chapter 6 of the *Tractatus*, Spinoza used this concept of natural law as a way of denying any supernatural or miraculous causes of events. Spinoza made clear that he did not *doubt* various miraculous explanations; he was going much further by *denying* the very possibility of them. As a law of nature is the divine way in which things operate and cannot be otherwise, a miracle would have to be a contravention of a law of nature. Spinoza, therefore, pushed the whole realm of supernatural explanation aside and at this point was ready to present his scientific way of studying Scripture.

Spinoza's so-called scientific explanation of the Bible had been preceded by a work by his friend and doctor Lodewijk Meyer. In *Philosophy, Interpreter of Holy Scripture*, Meyer offered a strictly rational evaluation of Scripture. Similarly, Spinoza presents what he is doing as much like that of a scientist studying nature. He says his method is almost the same; it involves studying the text in terms of its history, original meaning, effects, and so on. Spinoza says that he is going to interpret Scripture solely in terms of itself and to do this one has to know as much as possible about the original language, the authors, and their intentions.

It is interesting that Spinoza does not engage in what was then appearing as biblical scholarship – comparing manuscripts and editing texts – but, rather, seems to think he can explain Scripture by taking it at face value and asking what it means, who wrote it, and why. Spinoza pointed out that we are limited in reconstructing the Hebrew of biblical times since much of the language has disappeared. He raised skeptical problems about getting back to what a text meant long ago. The problem becomes more difficult when the language in which the text is written has only partially survived and there are questions as to what terms might have meant two thousand years earlier. Present-day Hebrew is not necessarily the same as ancient Hebrew so we can only guess as to what various terms or phrases might have meant then. Spinoza did not claim that there were any concepts that would stand out above and beyond the temporary language formulations. Later on, in the same section, he contended that one could understand Euclidean geometry no matter what language it was written in because one could understand the concepts in Greek or any other language. If the Bible contains only ordinary human musings about human subjects then the actual context has to be recaptured as much as possible. But Spinoza saw that after a range of 1500 years or so there was very limited possibility of doing this completely or thoroughly. Another order of skeptical problems arises from the transmission of the text as to whether we have the same text that was written down over two thousand years ago. This problem was developed at length by the Quaker Samuel Fisher. Both he and Spinoza argued that it is doubtful that the text could have survived copying and copying and copying without all kinds of additions, errors, and subtractions occurring.[84]

Another kind of skeptical problem is developed by Spinoza concerning the question of who wrote the Bible. The first five books are said to be written by Moses but, within these books, there is an account of the death of Moses and subsequent events. Thomas Hobbes and Isaac La Peyrère had made much of the difficult consequences of this. Spinoza, going back to Rabbi Abraham Ibn Ezra (1092–1167), points out that the text in Deuteronomy clearly indicates that someone other than Moses must have written the death scene and what happens thereafter.*

---

*The commentary of Ibn Ezra was printed alongside the biblical text in the Hebrew Bible published in Venice in the mid-sixteenth century. This Bible contains the commentaries of David Kimchi and Raschi.

Ibn Ezra did not see any startling conclusions to be drawn from considering the possibility that a few lines had been written by someone other than Moses. This did not denigrate the value of the text but, in fact, in his eyes, made the non-Mosaic lines of special interest and import. So he suggested studying them for their unique message.

Other commentators said that Moses could see the future and that he wept when he wrote his own death scene. Some took the mildly innovative step in saying that Aaron, the brother of Moses, wrote the lines in question, but none until the mid-seventeenth century saw any great problem. Hobbes claimed that Moses could only be considered the author of those passages that are strictly said to be by Moses. La Peyrère took the giant step of saying there must have been more than one author. Samuel Fisher, who was so concerned about the transmission problem, could see that all sorts of changes could have crept into the text over the centuries. He even offered some conspiratorial explanations; stubborn Jews might have wanted to change the text, and Catholics likewise, in order to keep their control. So Fisher would have accidental and purposeful multi authors.

Spinoza went on to elaborate on these biblical critics. For Spinoza, if there were lines not written by Moses, then another author wrote them and the Bible would have to have had at least two authors. Once this was granted, soon one would be in a world in which the biblical text could be considered a compilation of many hands at many times. It no longer had to be seen as something that had been set apart and preserved outside of time and place. Now it could be seen as writings of the ancient Hebrews over a period of time as they interacted with many forces and developments.

Thus, the question of who wrote the passage about Moses's death soon opens up a totally different perspective about what kind of document the Bible is and what sort of considerations should be given to its text. Spinoza had not destroyed previous ways of looking at the Bible but had offered a totally different way of looking at it. The Bible seen as a human achievement can then be evaluated in purely human terms. Like La Peyrère and Fisher, Spinoza saw that there were now great skeptical problems to be resolved before one could be sure who wrote the text and what the intention was.

Spinoza piled difficulty upon difficulty. He then attacked Maimonides who had sought to rationalize the Bible in order to overcome any problems. Making the text conform to reason was totally unnecessary, Spinoza contended; the text could just be what it was.

Maimonides is one of the very few Jewish philosophers whom Spinoza discusses. The twelfth-century philosopher-theologian had sought to make Judaism compatible with rational philosophy and to smooth over obvious conflicts of common sense with religious tradition. Maimonides had pointed out that there was no reason to expect that, when the messianic days would begin, the mountains would disappear and the world would become a plain sphere. Instead, Maimonides just took this as metaphorical and said the world would look exactly the same geographically and geologically before and after the messianic days but spiritually it would have been transformed. (This particular passage was censored by rabbis in the early thirteenth century and a copy in the synagogue library in Amsterdam contains this text with ink blotting it out.) Spinoza dismissed this as just rationalization and unnecessary. One could accept the biblical text as is and not have to worry about whether it fits with reason or not. Sometimes one has the feeling that Spinoza was yelling at Maimonides to get rid of this sort of religious rationalist compromise that the medieval rabbi was offering.[85]

Spinoza also attacked a minor medieval commentator, Rabbi Jehuda Alpakhar, for maintaining that reason must be accommodated to Scripture. Some people have suggested that Spinoza must have known all of the commentaries if he had found writings by the obscure Alpakhar. It has recently been discovered, however, that this particular text that Spinoza commented on had been printed by some Christian Hebraists in Hebrew and Latin in Spinoza's time and that this may be a comment on their views.

Spinoza's new way of looking at the Bible is a turning point in the development of biblical criticism. Before Spinoza, Hobbes and La Peyrère had raised questions about the biblical text but had still tried to conserve ways in which it could be accepted as a picture of how human beings came into the world and developed. Spinoza, in his questioning of whether we have an accurate text, was raising a much deeper question, namely, what is the cognitive value of the material that we possess? In conceptualizing what is discussed in the Bible, Spinoza loosened its connections to historical schemata: one could even question whether the events occurred but this no longer mattered if they were examined in context. In this, he was going beyond Thomas Hobbes, Isaac La Peyrère, and Samuel Fisher, who all accepted the special status of the Bible and were just trying to make sense of the document in its special status. La Peyrère probably came closest to what Spinoza was doing when he said in *Pre-Adamitae* that "Scripture is just a heap of copie of copie." La Peyrère was not denying that the Bible is a special document with special status; what he was denying was that the printed documents that publishers put out labeled as the Bible, and the parchment copies in libraries, are not the revealed text. They are human attempts to present the message in human terms and they are infected and infested with human failings. La Peyrère was impressed that one Protestant Bible scholar, Louis Cappel, had found that there were 7000 variants in the Greek Old Testament.

Spinoza began a more radical way of treating the material: what is being dealt with is a human production. We can ask: who wrote it, why was it written, what is one supposed to do about it? All these questions are about human affairs and can be studied in terms of human evidence. This transformation of the nature of the study of the Bible quickly turned it into a secular historical study. John Calvin had asked in the *Institutes*, how can one tell the difference between Titus Livy's history and the Bible? Calvin had decided one could only tell by a sort of private, personal revelation to the reader, which made him or her capable of reading the text as a religious text.[86] For Spinoza, there is only a secular text, and then one can ask, what was going on at the time? What did the words mean at the time? What sort of changes occurred in the document? And so on. Spinoza's transformation then launched the next three centuries of biblical criticism with a wide variety of results.

In the immediate scene, Hobbes, La Peyrère, and Spinoza were criticized together as an unholy Trinity that had been trying to destroy the biblical message. One of the first major biblical scholars to attempt to deal with this way of approaching the Scripture was Father Richard Simon, an Oratorian with a fantastic amount of erudition about ancient texts and the greatest Bible scholar of the next generation. His critical history of the Old Testament, which appeared in 1678, one year after Spinoza's death, said that he agreed with Spinoza's method but not his conclusion. The method freed the biblical text from any necessary connection with any events and allowed the examiner to put a spotlight on various ways text developed. Simon said that this did not preclude ultimately finding the accurate meaning of the Bible. It meant that one would have to go through an enormous, possibly infinite, number of steps in trying to get from a presently human text to a superhuman, supernatural text. Simon, knowing much more about the linguistic and historical problems than Spinoza, then set out programs that would have to be gone through before any definitive judgment could be made as to what the Bible said or meant. The last three centuries of Bible scholarship, at least the liberal sort, has tried to operate within these parameters.[87]

Simon's many volumes uncovered more and more layers of the human side but never seemed to cross the epistemological gulf to get to the divine side. Simon insisted that, unlike Spinoza, he was not trying to demote the status of the Bible. He was just trying to do the spadework needed before one could find the pure message. He was denounced by many Protestant scholars as causing a skepticism with regard to religion and he was severely criticized by his church, which took away his post, his pulpit, and finally left him a defrocked priest without a diocese.

Spinoza and Simon played a very great role in the development of modern Bible scholarship. It is of some interest that one of the first Bible scholars to adopt the Spinoza/Simon way of considering the Bible was the great scientist Isaac Newton. Newton follows their critiques and treats the Bible, as we know it, as a human production that probably got mixed up many ways in the last thousand years. He even suggests that various pages of the Book of Samuel fell on the floor and got reassembled in a careless manner. Other scholars were suggesting that some of the books were not biblical but human productions that got included in the original corpus. Still others suggested that all sorts of additions were made over time and that other works disappeared. So it was probably not possible to find the pure message but only to approximate it to some degree.

From his analysis of Scripture as an object to be evaluated historically and textually, Spinoza then considers its cognitive value for modern society. While Spinoza asserts that it has no truths that cannot be known independently from careful study and reasoning, Scripture can make people accept and obey some basic moral principles. These are found by careful reasoning with or without any reference to the Bible. Spinoza lists these principles under seven headings as a kind of basic religion for rational people:

1. "God, or a Supreme Being, exists";
2. "God is One";
3. God "is omnipresent";
4. God has "supreme right and dominion over all things" and "does nothing under compulsion," only by "fiat and grace";
5. The "worship of God consists only in justice and charity, or love towards one's neighbor";

6.   All "who obey God by their manner of life are saved"; and
7.   God "forgives the sins of those who repent."

Spinoza offers several possibilities as to how one can understand God, including the Quaker belief that God is light.

These rules are not offered as statements cut into parchment centuries ago but as views that a rational person in the mid-seventeenth century would find made reasonable sense. Thus one did not need an ancient text to justify these views but simply to clarify perceptions at the present time.

For Spinoza the critical point is what leads people to obey universal moral law as exemplified in the proposition, "do unto others as you would have them do unto you." Purely rational people will comprehend that this is the way people must act if they want to live in a harmonious society. People who do not have the rational ability to reach this conclusion are led to obey by the force of scriptural text. Thus, for Spinoza, the role of traditional and organized religion becomes one of keeping people in a moral world whether they understand it or not. Religion becomes subservient to political-social policy and when reduced to this position it can then play an important role *as long as it stays within its legitimate bounds.*

Spinoza's reduction of the role of religion to that of producing civil obedience made it easier for him to envisage toleration of almost any religious group as long as its members adhered to the moral principle to "love thy neighbor as thyself." Others at the time were worried about whether a more tolerant society could countenance deviant Christian views or even non-Christian views. There were disputes as to whether Quakers, Socinians, and other kinds of Christian heretics could be tolerated. In practice, the Netherlands became a living theater for these many types of religious outlooks and it became clear that they could all live together as long as they tolerated each other. The Socinians, who had developed a movement in Poland, became refugees in the Netherlands in the 1660s and 1670s. Spinoza knew at least one of their leaders. The Quakers had been in Amsterdam since the mid

1650s. A not-too-disguised Catholic Church carried on and various English non-conformist groups were part of the scene as well. There was also a small Muslim population in addition to the burgeoning and flourishing Jewish one. The main threat, from a political point of view, was that of the more rigidly orthodox Calvinists trying to force their views on the state. But Spinoza's attitude was more or less representative of the state. Henri Méchoulan has suggested that there was a constant balancing act between the desire for freedom and the desire for money and that the Dutch managed to create a society in which most people could profit economically regardless of their religious views and, at the same time, their religious views could exist side by side with those who held radically different ones.[88]

What was considered the text case in the discussion on toleration was whether a society could tolerate an atheist. It was presumed that a person would only do good or do the right thing from fear of future punishment. If there were no fear of punishment beyond the grave what would stop atheists from robbing, killing, raping, and so on? In Spinoza's account, anyone who saw the truth of the moral law and acted accordingly could be accepted as a member of society, thus there was no reason to fear the atheist if he or she understood the grounds of morality. It is interesting in this respect that, just a few years after Spinoza's death, Pierre Bayle advanced the shocking thesis that a society of atheists could be more moral than a society of Christians. His stock example of the moral atheist was the now-deceased Baruch Spinoza whom Bayle painted as a moral saint and a systematic atheist. Bayle carried this to the extreme, maintaining that most Christians did not believe their religious views and acted out of non-religious drives and hence Christian societies were corrupt to the core. Bayle sought to show that leaders of various factions of Christianity had committed terrible acts, as had the leaders of Judaism in ancient times. The things they did were not the result of their religion but the result of their humanity. Human depravity, Bayle contended, had existed from the earliest records of mankind to the present. People were not dissuaded of their bad impulses because of possible punishment in another life.

Bayle tried to offer a comparable study of atheists and non-atheists. He offered a few ancient Greek atheists and Spinoza as examples of fine moral people and in contrast wrote horror stories about ancient biblical figures, Renaissance popes, and recent Protestant leaders. It was obvious to both Bayle and Spinoza that morality did not depend on people's fear of an afterlife. Moral decisions are made here and now and affect present events even though there is no meaning in Spinoza's world for an individual life after death. Humans are capable of virtuous activities in terms of how they will events and evaluate events, even though they cannot cause them, and it is human intellectual decisions that determine human morality.

Since, for Spinoza, moral actions go on in historical time, it is in the social and political sphere that they are evaluated. This is why the political society is more important for Spinoza than any religious organization. The latter, no matter how they may consider themselves, in fact are acting as part of the moral apparatus of the state if they are teaching people to obey. If they are not, then they are immoral and should be treated as such.

Spinoza's interpretation of the Bible, as a human production of ancient times whose present relevance was mainly to lead people to obey moral laws, became a way of explaining the nature of political society and the role of intellectual and religious activity within society. In chapter 16 of the *Tractatus*, Spinoza contends that what leads people to join together in political society is their need for protection from each other. Spinoza starts from a picture somewhat like Hobbes's in the *Leviathan*. The basic human condition may not be as cruel as Hobbes's war of all against all, but in Spinoza's philosophy people get in each other's way and desire the same objects. This leads to strife on many different levels. Rational people realize that they can only survive in this situation if they are protected by a force that is able to control everyone. Thus they cede their own individual liberty to a sovereign in exchange for this protection; those people who are not able to make this rational judgment must be forced into a controlled social position. The state emerges as the vehicle that makes human coexistence possible. Spinoza is willing to go further than Hobbes in ceding complete power to the sovereign. However, he also realizes that the sovereign could misuse this power for selfish and personal gratification that has nothing to do with protecting the well being of his subjects. Spinoza does not try to specify limits to state sovereignty but he makes the observation that any ruler or rulers who abuse their power will soon be overthrown and this would again endanger everyone until another stable society is formed.

Isolating some of Spinoza's ideas on the role of the sovereign has prompted some critics to see him as the forerunner of the modern totalitarian state. Others see him as wavering between the peace that can be provided by a strong monarch and the suppression that will possibly result from such a central political authority. Spinoza's views here probably reflect what was actually going on in the political life of the Netherlands at the time. In the course of the century, theoretical problems about limiting the power of the sovereign were acted out as the political scene changed. The society moved between a very limited and loose federation of provinces to a strong central government. Thus, an observer like Spinoza could see in practice what could happen and what was happening in a new governmental experiment that was taking place. He also seems to have followed fairly closely what was happening in England, from the Puritan revolution through the Restoration. Based on these observations, he seems to have come to the view that there should be no limit on the sovereign's power, but that any sovereign with any sense would see that there is nothing to be gained from abusing the power and that the most likely outcome of an abuse would be a social revolution to overthrow the sovereign. In the last year of his life Spinoza wrote the *Political Treatise* that dealt with an examination of constitutions and workings of various forms of government – monarchy, aristocracy, and democracy – and he made clear his preference for a democratic republican authority.

The end of the *Tractatus* centers on preserving individual freedom to think as one pleases. By making them subservient to the state Spinoza had tried to limit the possibility of censorship by religious organizations. He also wanted to limit the state's control of intellectuals, arguing that there is really nothing the state can do or should do to limit intellectual activity. In this respect, Spinoza has been seen as a precursor of the civil toleration that developed in the eighteenth century, especially in the newly formed United States.

Spinoza realized, no doubt, the revolutionary perspective he was offering in the *Tractatus*. In the preface to his *Tractatus Theologico-Politicus* he sought to present himself as a mild, meek investigator who, as a human being, was doing the best he could. He said at the end of the preface and also at the end of the book that if the society thought there was any danger in what he was writing he would be glad to make adjustments – which he never did, however, even after the book was condemned.

The *Tractatus* appeared anonymously in Latin in 1670 with the title page indicating that it had been published in Germany. This ruse delayed, but did not prevent, censorship by the Dutch authorities. The *Tractatus* was also published in several editions in the same year. Jonathan Israel has given us an amazing picture both of how it was published and how it became a best seller all over the western world within a few years.[89] Groups within the Dutch and French Reformed Church in the Netherlands were properly shocked and denounced the book and sought to have it banned. The liberal government that existed under Jan de Witt had tried to ignore the many, many attempts of censorship of numerous other writings pressed for by leaders of the Reformed churches. De Witt had been alerted to the Spinoza problem and tried to avoid coming in contact with the author or giving any support to his book, while at the same time preventing the reintroduction of censorship. Two years after publication, Colonel

Jean-Baptiste Stouppe, in his *La Religion des Hollandois*, complained that nobody in the Netherlands had written a refutation of Spinoza and the book was freely available. A Professor von Mansfeld was reported to be working on a refutation but it did not appear for several years due to the author's illness and death. The various synods of Reformed groups kept pressing for a ban and sometimes achieved local success but a countrywide ban did not occur until after de Witt was removed from office and killed in 1674. Even after this, one could purchase copies without too much trouble and the work was widely distributed in the Netherlands and elsewhere. One finds comments about it in works by such English authors as Henry More, Ralph Cudworth, and Robert Boyle.

The furor over the publication of the *Tractatus* should be put in perspective. There had been a tradition for at least a century of clandestine publication coming out of the Low Countries. The famous Plantin Presse in Antwerp had been printing Protestant religious materials to be sent to Spain with false title pages, misleading indices, and so on. In the seventeenth century, the Dutch publishers became the leading printers in Europe and some were very adept at getting their products past any form of censorship. Semi collusion between the publishers and the authorities often circumvented any ardent attempt at banning publications. Authors even became adept at sneaking material into ordinary works. For example, the publisher Pierre Desmaizeaux created a fake letter by Pierre Bayle to be included in the 1715 edition of Bayle's letters. The fake letter gave reports that Desmaizeaux had received from Spinoza's friend Henri Morelli about Spinoza's views. In Desmaizeaux's letters one finds he was attempting to publish around the same time an *éloge* to Spinoza. The publisher Prosper Marchand was astute enough to ward off publication of the text, which is now, unfortunately, lost.

Criticisms of the *Tractatus* occurred quickly, both in the Netherlands and abroad. The emphasis on the irreligious implications of his thought seems to have been predominant.

However, he was also seen as a follower of Descartes who had pushed Cartesian theory to a new model in which everything could be explained by one and only one substance, God. Various Cartesian thinkers at the end of the seventeenth and the beginning of the eighteenth century saw dangerous implications in spinozistic Cartesianism. They saw that it would immediately lead to an unorthodox pantheism. Spinoza's influence among the Cartesians was partly in making clear the need for consistently following out Descartes's doctrine of substance while guarding against the constant possibility that this would open the door to pantheism and to a non-Christian religion. When told about Spinoza's *Tractatus*, the Cambridge Platonist Henry More said that he knew it would happen that a Cartesian would become an atheist and that serious scholars would have to refute this new development. Spinoza's atheism and his pantheism are discussed in the last decades of the seventeenth century by More and Ralph Cudworth, both negatively.[90] Father Nicolas Malebranche, perhaps the leading Cartesian at the end of the seventeenth century, was accused of spinozism and spent much time trying to show that his theory of intelligible extension in no way amounted to the same metaphysical theory as that of Spinoza.

Chapter Seven

The *Ethics*

From 1661 onward, along with these other projects, Spinoza had been working on his masterpiece, the *Ethics*, in geometrical form. He seems to have found this method an exciting way to present philosophy without any misunderstandings, strictly in terms of accepted truths and rational demonstrations. No footnotes or citations of authorities were necessary. Hence, Spinoza used the geometrical method (see p. 50) as a way of clarifying his differences with Descartes and, above all, as a way of presenting his own philosophy in the *Ethics*, which he finally completed in 1675.

From his correspondence we can see this ongoing project developing and reaching completion. Resulting in its being banned, there had been such an outcry against the *Tractatus* that Spinoza decided to forgo the pleasure of seeing the *Ethics* published in his lifetime lest it cause even more opposition. He set it aside, making careful arrangements for it to be published shortly after his demise.

There is no introduction to the *Ethics* and the name of the author is only given with the initials BDS. The reader of the work who knows geometry starts with the definitions and the axioms and then can study the derivation of the theorems. As we shall see, this austere, strictly geometrical presentation soon requires some additional data in the form of notes and explanations. As the work unfolds, more and more expository material appears to make sure the reader has grasped the point. Clues that might have helped, such as references to other philosophies, are rare, leaving it to later scholars to find possible sources of various items that occur in the development.

It is amazing that the core of Spinoza's metaphysics is worked out in Part 1 in the first fifteen propositions, covering ten pages. Spinoza's pantheism is then presented as the stark conclusion to the logical examination of what follows from the nature of substance. Starting from some definitions of substance – God, attribute, mode, that which is self-caused, and that which is finite in its own kind – Spinoza then, in a series of very short proofs, establishes that God as substance necessarily exists. In proposition 14 Spinoza writes that "there can be, or be conceived, no other substance but God," and in proposition 15, "whatever is, is in God, and nothing can be or be conceived without God."[91] I shall comment on the logical sequence from the definitions to these monumental conclusions later on. Right now I should like to discuss the strong pantheistic cosmology that is presented here.

There has been a long tradition in philosophy and in Judeo-Christian theology of trying to explain the world in terms of what its causes may be, tracing it back to being an effect from an all-powerful deity. Spinoza's reading abolishes any distinction between the cause and the effect. Whatever is, is God and is in God. One finds antecedents of this in some of the Neoplatonic and mystical Jewish, Christian, and Muslim philosophers from John Scotus Erigena, Solomon Ibn Gabirol, St. Bonaventura, and Meister Eckhart. A new and powerful form of some of this emerged in the sixteenth century with the philosopher-poet Leone Ebreo and the philosopher-physicist Giordano Bruno. This pantheism seemed to swallow up all distinction between God and the world and to make the doctrine of Creation meaningless. Bruno, whom Spinoza read, was burned at the stake in

1600 for his wild pantheistic proposals that seemed to make a mockery of the Church and its doctrines. There was also a pantheistic stream coming out of the new kabbalistic literature from the school of Isaac Luria. Luria's views were known to a few people in Amsterdam through Abraham Cohen Herrera, who had been the first European to study them when one of Luria's disciples was teaching in Dubrovnik. After many adventures in the world, Herrera settled in Amsterdam when the Jewish community was at its beginning and lived quietly there until his death in 1635. He wrote two logic texts, one of which has his Christian name, Alonso Núñez de Herrera, which suggests that he had a Christian audience in mind. Spinoza used some material from Herrera's main exposition of kabbalism, *Puerta del cielo*, in the *Ethics*, although we do not know whether he gained it from the Spanish or the Hebrew version. At any rate, there was a current kabbalistic school in Amsterdam and some of the views advanced had strong pantheistic tendencies. One further possible source was the teachings of the German mystic Jacob Boehme. Boehme, a shoemaker, presented a mystical view of God entwined in the physical universe. Boehme's views attracted a lot of interest among seventeenth-century intellectuals as providing possible bases for a new understanding of the natural and the divine world.[92]

Spinoza's version is possibly the strongest statement of pantheism of the time with no sign of mystical overtones. However, from his early days onward he was in a milieu where kabbalistic ideas in Jewish and Christian forms were being taken seriously. It seems likely that he was aware of this and was treading his way through a world in which the same phenomena were being explained in both kabbalistic and what we would now call scientific terms. Spinoza's *Ethics* was published in 1677, the same year that the *Kabbalah Denudata* was published, both by the same firm in Amsterdam. The *Kabbalah Denudata* was a collection of different sixteenth- and seventeeth-century kabbalistic texts translated into Latin. The first in the collection is

Puerta del cielo by Herrera, who had been the teacher of both Isaac Aboab de Fonseca and Menasseh ben Israel. This collection was read by many authors, including Locke, Leibniz, and Newton, among others.

Spinoza comments, at one point, that the kabbalists are just a group of triflers "whose madness passes the bounds of my understanding."[93] The context indicates that Spinoza really objected to the people who were finding all sorts of divine clues in the numerology, typography, and diacritical signs in the biblical text. He also found that the readings these kabbalistic triflers made proceeded "from folly and a feebleminded devoutness or from arrogance and malice, to the end that they alone may be credited with possessing the secrets of God." Far from uncovering such secrets, their writings were "mere child-ishness."[94] Because of these passages, it has been assumed that he had no interest or sympathy with these people. Yet, although Spinoza made negative comments about the kabbalists he knew, it is interesting that as soon as the *Ethics* was published one of the first interpretations of what he was doing was that he was following out kabbalistic interpretations in Cartesian terms. The first readers associated what they found in Spinoza's text with Herrera. In the critiques by Jacques Basnage and Johann Georg Wachter a comparison is made of Spinoza's basic approach with that of Herrera's and the same criticisms are made of both.[95] Around 1700, Basnage, who was writing the first history of the Jews in modern times, asked one of the leading rabbis of Amsterdam what he made of Spinoza's views. The unnamed rabbi – probably Isaac Aboab de Fonseca – told him that Spinoza plagiarized the views of the kabbalists and tried to make himself appear original by casting this in Cartesian terminology. Wachter, a philosophical theologian, had come to Amsterdam to see an old friend Peter Spaeth, who had turned from being a pietist to joining a Jewish community, adopting the name Moses Germanus. Wachter discovered from his conversations with his friend that there was a pantheistic kabbalism that was developed from the texts that were included in the *Kabbalah Denudata* and that this was the same as a central portion of Spinoza's metaphysics. Wachter went further and claimed that this sort of kabbalistic spinozism had been part of Judaism from antiquity to the present. Both Wachter and Basnage seem to have taken the emanation theory in the Kabbalah as the same sort of theory of neo-Platonism that appears in Spinoza's view of the nature of God as being the sole entity in the universe from which all things are manifestations.

Spinoza, when read in terms of what he himself called the first and second kind of knowledge, looks like a super-consistent Cartesian who has overcome various inconsistencies in Descartes and has developed a one-substance theory to account for the new knowledge of the scientific era. But Spinoza, when looked at in terms of what he called the third kind of knowledge, can be read as a rational kabbalist shorn of its imagery and numerology. Spinoza may have been attracted to the philosophical kabbalism of Herrera or at least was willing to use something of it without taking anything from what he regarded as the lunatic fringe of kabbalism. This kabbalistic interpretation seems to have disappeared as more and more emphasis was placed by late seventeenth- and early eighteenth-century readers on Spinoza's rationalist and anti-religious views.

Spinoza had been working for years in the Cartesian mode of explanation. He saw the logical mathematical side of it as one of the most fruitful ways of leading man to understand the world. He also saw that Descartes's three-substance theory would not hold up once one logically analyzed what a substance was and could do. From a journey through Cartesianism, Spinoza realized that Descartes's philosophy had to be reduced to a form of pantheism and hence came to the great pantheistic utterance that everything is in God and is God. According to Descartes, God was the only creative power in the world and God was all-powerful. What could the world be but an extension of God? Could there be separate aspects of the world called Mind and

Matter? Spinoza answers with a resounding no, since everything has to be explained by God and therefore has to be, in some sense, part of God.

Philosophy from ancient times to the present has endeavored to explain human experience in terms of some underlying features of the universe. Over centuries, theories have been advanced that describe sense experience by explaining the natural world behind it. Then, a causal framework that explains the natural world is worked out, attributing it to a creator God who had the power to bring all this into existence. In the history of philosophy one major current emerging principally from Plato and Neoplatonism is the attempt to understand the world as an emanation from this all-powerful divine being, in contrast to theories that contend that God created the natural world *ex nihilo*, out of nothing. The emanationist theories have the problem of accounting for any separate existence of the emanated beings. If there is no difference, then this becomes a form of pantheism. If there is a difference, then what is it that really separates God from the world and is it possible that the world can have an independent existence? Descartes, and then Spinoza, start with a conception of God as an all-powerful and infinite being, the creator of all things. Can the created material world or the mental world actually be different from the creator? And if different, what can be the substantial difference – what can the world be made of that would be different from its creator source? Spinoza uses the logic entailed by the notion of an all-powerful being to show that there cannot be any separate, created world. If one goes back to the outset of the *Ethics*, the definitions concerning God are as follows:

1. By that which is self-caused I mean that whose essence involves existence; or that whose nature can be conceived only as existing.
2. A thing is said to be finite in its own kind (*in suo genere finita*) when it can be limited by another thing of the same nature. For example, a body is said to be finite because we

can always conceive of another body greater than it. So, too, a thought is limited by another thought. But body is not limited by thought, nor thought by body.

3. By substance I mean that which is in itself and is conceived through itself; that is, that the conception of which does not require the conception of another thing from which it has to be formed.

4. By attribute I mean that which the intellect perceives of substance as constituting its essence.

5. By mode I mean the affections of substance; that is, that which is in something else and is conceived through something else.

6. By God I mean an absolutely infinite being; that is, substance consisting of infinite attributes, each of which expresses eternal and infinite essence.[96]

Proposition 1 states "substance is by nature prior to its affections." This, as Spinoza points out, is an immediate consequence of the definition of substance. Proposition 2 claims that "two substances having different attributes have nothing in common." Spinoza points out that this follows from the definition of substance, that it is conceived through itself and thus cannot be conceived or understood through anything else. Proposition 3 says that "when things have nothing in common, one cannot be the cause of the other." This proposition, Spinoza shows, is an immediate consequence of two of his axioms, 4 and 5, which declare that "the knowledge of an effect depends on, and involves, the knowledge of the cause" and "things which have nothing in common with each other cannot be understood through each other; that is, the conception of the one does not involve the conception of the other." Proposition 4 states that "two or more distinct things are distinguished from one another either by the difference of the attributes of the substances or by the difference of the affections of the substances," while proposition 5 says that "in the universe there cannot be two or more substances of the same nature or attribute." This proposition, which is crucial for what follows, is presented as quickly following from the definitions and axioms. Proposition 6 states that "one substance cannot be produced by another substance." Since substances are the cause of themselves it is obvious that one cannot have productive causality of one substance from another. This obviates the Cartesian claim that there can be separate substances of God, Matter and Mind with the latter two produced by the former. Proposition 7 claims that "existence belongs to the nature of substance," and Proposition 8 says that "every substance is necessarily infinite." If not, substance could be acted upon or limited by something else. This quickly leads to Spinoza pointing out that in his axiom system God has infinite attributes and that God by definition necessarily exists. Proposition 11, which makes this assertion, is probably the purest form of the ontological argument for the existence of God that has been offered in the history of philosophy. The ontological argument was presented in the Middle Ages by St. Anselm (1033–1109) who contended that anyone who knew the definition of God knew that he necessarily exists. Even the fool who denies God's existence will recognize his mistake if he thinks about what is entailed by the notion of a perfect being, namely, a being that has complete reality including existence. A somewhat similar version was offered by Descartes in the fifth *Meditation*. Earlier, Descartes had offered a causal proof for the existence of God but in *Meditation V* he said that mere examination of the definition would allow one to see it was part of the nature of God to exist, just as it is part of the nature of a valley to be next to a mountain. Spinoza's version is the most succinct and cites the definition of God and the propositions about substance necessarily existing.

It should be noted that the ontological argument has been found unconvincing as a way of answering the question of whether a God that can intervene in human affairs actually exists. Blaise Pascal, Spinoza's French contemporary, found that the god of the philosophers was of no particular interest. The God he was seeking and found was the God of Abraham, Isaac and Jacob.

Spinoza does not propose the argument as having any relevance to any religious quest. He was clarifying the logical implications of the terms "God" and "Substance" that he had started with in his system. He goes on from this to point out that within his system there cannot be any distinction between God and nature since nature cannot be a separate existence – hence the great pantheistic conclusion.

Let us stop for a moment. Readers may say this is all fun and games, but what does it prove? Spinoza starts with a slew of axioms and definitions and shuffles them around like a man doing card tricks and comes up with these monumental conclusions. His system would not have impressed anybody unless the definitions were the same as or close to what other philosophers had accepted and the same is true with his axioms. But, the reader is still saying, even if there is nothing implausible, why accept Spinoza's version as the correct one? If one is willing to grant that Spinoza's ideas could be considered as true ideas then "a true idea must agree with that of which it is the idea."[97] This supposedly is the guarantee that Spinoza's world of ideas is about the actual world. This is not proven in any form, manner, or shape but simply asserted in Axiom 6.

Spinoza was aware that proposition 14 would run counter to most people's conception of divinity. Instead of just ploughing on with the logic of the situation, Spinoza felt it necessary to introduce a scholium here in which he contrasted popular views about the deity with God in the spinozistic system. It is obvious from the very definition of God and mode (mode being any kind of modification of God, finite or infinite) that anything that has parts cannot be God and anything that is limited cannot be God. Hence, God cannot have any corporeal features. The fifteenth proposition declares a completely pantheistic world, not as a mystical moment but as the logical consequence of there being only one substance in the world. Once this is accepted, where could any entity be? It must be in the divine substance and must be perceived as some sort of modification or mode of the divine substance. The divine substance can only be thought of in terms of two of its infinite attributes – thought and extension. This is not because of any defect in the divine substance, which has infinite attributes, but because of limitations on the human observer who is only capable of conceiving God or substance in these two ways. It should be noted that Spinoza does not give substantial status to attributes. They are defined as ways in which substance is conceived.

Spinoza's world as he works out the logic of the last half of Part 1 of the *Ethics* is a necessarily determined state of affairs. Everything that happens, happens necessarily from the nature of God or substance. Nothing can be other than it is. God or nature acts from the necessary structure of its own being. This picture that Spinoza portrays is much like the world of the ancient Stoics. There is no contingency; there can be no new initiatives or changes of the course of events. Every event can be tracked back to a cause, which can be tracked back to a cause, and so on.

The universe can be seen as nature in two aspects, *natura naturans* and *natura naturata* (nature creating and nature created). The first relates to all that necessarily follows from the nature of God and the latter to the effects of God's nature. Thus, presumably, one can work out the necessary laws of the divine substance and causal explanations of the creative modes that follow from, and are in, the divine substance. Part 1 of Spinoza's *Ethics* gives a wonderful picture of this totally deterministic, pantheistic world. If one does not want to accept Spinoza's universe, then it is necessary to refute the logic of the situation.

At this point, having concluded the propositions that detail the nature of God and the effects of the nature of God, Spinoza may have wondered if his readers would get the point that this is not just an exercise in logic but is a brutal challenge to popular religious belief. To spell this out, in the appendix to Part 1 Spinoza drops all pretense of the geometrical method and offers us a very strong statement regarding his views about superstition and popular religion. He saw the popular interpretation of what goes on in the world as based on reading purposes into events and especially human purposes. Without knowing the causes of events people have been most concerned to figure out what ends are being achieved. Then they construct teleological explanations in which forces beyond man are acting to aid or abet or to chastise and hinder human activity. As people coupled this quest for purposeful explanation with the conviction that there was an all-powerful controlling force in the world, they began to fret about the problem of evil. How can it be that an all-powerful being would allow such bad things to happen? And, if added to this was the conviction that the all-powerful being was also all-good then the mystery grew much greater. However, if one examined the sort of events that illustrate the problem of evil in scientific terms, one would see that the events are physically caused according to laws of nature. They are not aimed at good or bad purposes but are part of the way the world operates. Earthquakes, volcanoes, and tidal waves are the result of natural forces; in certain cases they have very unfortunate consequences for some people but they may also have good consequences for others. But neither the good nor the bad consequences are intended; they happen because that is the way of nature. To insist on an explanation of this in terms of the malevolence or benefi-cence of the forces that control nature is to make nonsense out of what is actually going on.

Spinoza suggested that this sort of superstitious reading of the world would have continued indefinitely if it were not for the emergence of mathematical reasoning. The latter provided clear and definite explanations for natural occurrences without any regard to purpose or final cause, so that Spinoza, by following the geometrical method, was able to portray a world without any distortions.

Ignorant people who are so concerned with a purposeful world are also concerned about how things and events relate to themselves. They therefore start impugning value character-istics to objects that affect them and speak of them as good, bad, ugly, beautiful, and so on. If they kept to a rational mathematical description of things none of this would happen. Instead, they have made the world as mad as themselves and each person has ended up with a personalized view of events and no one knows what to truly believe. The implication is that they should follow Spinoza's path and only apply the mathematical method to the understanding of events, which is what he proceeds to do in Part 2.

Spinoza moves on to develop his theory of how mental and physical events take place. The second part of the *Ethics* starts with the definition of idea and body. The first he describes as "a conception of the Mind which the Mind forms because it is a thinking thing." The body is "a mode that expresses in a definite and determinate way God's essence in so far as he is considered as an extended thing."[98] It is important to recall that Spinoza's statement of extension as being one of the attributes by which nature is known is also presented with a denial that extension can be divided. Spinoza's material world does not have corpuscles or atoms but is an extended plenum through which nature is understood. At the time that Spinoza was working this out there were serious attempts to explain events in terms of a modernized form of ancient atomism. An older contemporary of Spinoza's, Pierre Gassendi, had presented the atomism of Epicurus as a framework for understanding modern physics. Spinoza rejected this conception of discrete portions of matter being active forces. In developing the background for his physical theory one of the most important features is what appears in proposition 7: "The order and connection of ideas is the same as the order and connection of things." Spinoza explains this in his scholium:

> whatever can be perceived by infinite intellect as constituting the essence of substance pertains entirely to the one sole substance. Consequently, thinking substance and extended substance are one and the same substance, comprehended now under this attribute, now under that. So, too, a mode of Extension and the idea of that mode are one and the same thing, expressed in two ways.[99]

Here Spinoza introduces one of his radical innovations to seventeenth-century thought. For Descartes, matter and mind are two totally separate creations of the deity. Each is governed by its own laws and, as mentioned previously, there is an unsolved problem dealing with how two such totally disparate substances can interact. Cartesian dualism was leading Spinoza's contemporaries to stranger and stranger theories, such as occasionalism in which God is the only actor and God produces physical events on the occasion of mental events and mental events on the occasion of physical events, though there is no connection between the physical and mental events. Thus, a finger pressed on a piano key is the occasion for God to create a sound; the thought of playing a certain piano key becomes the occasion for God pressing a finger on the piano.

Leibniz, who was just beginning his public philosophical career in the mid-1670s, offered a totally different explanation – that of the pre-established harmony between mental and physical events. In Leibniz's theory there is no connection whatsoever between the physical and mental world; each has been created from the outset with a pre-established harmony with the other. When a finger is pressed on a doorbell, though there is no connection, a sound is heard because of the pre-established harmony. Neither Malebranche's nor Leibniz's theory seemed credible to readers at the time. Spinoza's solution, sometimes called psycho-physical parallelism, provides a seemingly easy solution. Any event can be seen in two ways – as physical or mental (there are also an infinite number of other ways these could be seen if we know other attributes of God). The two ways we see any event do not indicate they are two separate events. Instead, there are just two ways of looking at the situation.

The present-day discussion about whether computers think, whether one can create artificial intelligence, and whether the mind is the brain in its various functions, have revived interest in possible resolutions to the mind/body problem.[100] Some people in the field have been advocating something like Hobbes's view, namely, that all events are physical and caused by physical motions but that there is an epiphenomenal mental effect that comes along with the physical events. This epiphenomenal addition has no causal efficacy. It is something like the fragrance of a flower or the smell of something cooking. This interpretation tends to make all events physical. Its opponents insist on the unique character of mental experience as different from a series of physical events. This spinozistic theory could preserve the integrity of the mental experience along with the physical events in that they are the same set of events seen in two different ways. One does not have to explain the other; in fact, one cannot explain the other. But either one of them is a valid and important way of describing the state of affairs.

Thus, in the present debates about neurophysiological explanations of consciousness, Spinoza's view would obviate the dispute. On the one hand, people contend that consciousness is a feature of the physical brain states; on the other, that consciousness has to be understood independently, or apart, from the temporally conjoined events in the brain. Spinoza's dual-aspect theory would allow for both accounts to be simultaneously true – two ways of expressing the same state of affairs in one of the many modes of God.

Another debate along the same lines is whether mental illness should be treated physically or mentally. Psychiatrists and psychologists for the last fifty years or more have been looking for pharmaceutical ways of treating various mental disorders. Psychoanalysts have been resisting this and contending that some sort of mental contact, talk-therapy, is the way to deal with these problems. The contrast and conflict between these approaches has often led hospitals and other treatment centers to offer one of these possibilities while insisting that the other is quackery or illusion. A spinozistic reading would allow both to be ways of dealing with basically the same events. Medication and ideational treatment could both be ways of influencing certain behaviors and attitudes. On the spinozistic reading it would be the same situation that was being treated physically and/or mentally. One could work out causal studies of either the physical or the mental approach and neither has to be seen as conflicting with or contradicting the other.

Towards the end of Part 2 of the *Ethics* Spinoza evaluated the kinds of knowledge and certainty that could come out of such studies, providing a framework for developing a modern scientific account of what was going on in the world in terms of physical or mental modes. This amounts to a way of underpinning the structure of modern physical science. Unlike Descartes, for whom the defeat of skepticism had to be a prelude to discovering true knowledge, for Spinoza it is a relatively simple evaluation of what has been accomplished when one has true knowledge. Descartes could make it a cosmic struggle with evil demons, deceiving gods, and other horrendous possibilities that had to be eliminated before one could say that one had true and certain knowledge. For Spinoza, it was just a matter of looking at the knowledge we have, then one will see that skepticism was not a real possibility for intelligent people; it is either ignorance or stupidity. Proposition 43 states "He, who has a true idea, simultaneously knows that he has a true idea, and cannot doubt of the truth of the thing perceived." In a note to this proposition, Spinoza said,

> For nobody who has a true idea is unaware that a true idea involves absolute certainty. To have a true idea means only to know a thing perfectly, that is, to the utmost degree. Indeed, nobody can doubt this, unless he thinks that an idea is some dumb thing like a picture on a tablet, and not a mode of thinking, to wit, the very act of understanding. And who, pray, can know that he understands something unless he first understands it? That is, who can know that he is certain of something unless he is first certain of it? Again, what standard of truth can there be that is clearer and more certain than a true idea? Indeed, just as light makes manifest both itself and darkness, so truth is the standard both of itself and falsity.[101]

Spinoza disposed of one of the basic issues that generated skepticism that Descartes tried to overcome. An idea is not a lifeless object that one tries to evaluate by criteria, which themselves require justification. Spinoza insisted an idea is a mode of thinking whose truth or falsity shows itself. No infinite regress of methods is required, because having a true idea is the same as knowing something perfectly, and this shows itself from the natural faculties of the intellect. There is no possible skeptical problem because one knows, and knows that one knows, or one is in ignorance. The skeptic who wants to debate Spinoza will just be sent to contemplate whether he knows or understands something perfectly (which amounts to clear and certain knowledge). If the skeptic doubts whether he has such knowledge, he is then dismissed as an ignoramus who does not know what is essential to the debate.

For Spinoza, no long elaborate proof against the skeptics is needed since he is claiming, contrary to Descartes, that the very act of understanding as such makes one aware that he knows, and knows that he knows. Though the skeptic claims that such a person could be mistaken, Spinoza insisted this would be impossible if the person had a clear and certain idea. It would be its own criterion. The choice for Spinoza is either knowing God and all that follows from that knowledge, or knowing nothing. Since we know something, like a triangle is equal to two right angles, a truth that shows itself in the act of knowing it, we do not have to bother with skepticism, but rather with analyzing our truth to discover what makes it true, namely God. The skeptic knows nothing as he has all his purported doubts. He is in a state of ignorance which only a genuine knowing experience could cure. He may be in the state of suspending judgment, which means "that he is not adequately perceiving the thing."[102] As soon as he does he will give up his skepticism.

Spinoza did not see skepticism as the spectre haunting European philosophy. Unlike Descartes, who had to fight his way through skepticism to arrive at dogmatic truth, Spinoza simply began with an assurance that his system was true, and anyone who did not see this was either truth-blind (like colorblind) or was an ignoramus. The ignoramus can be helped if he can improve his understanding, and know something clearly and certainly, or adequately.

Spinoza's epistemological dogmatism is probably the furthest removed from skepticism of any of the new philosophies of the seventeenth century. It is a genuine anti-skeptical theory trying to eradicate the possibility or meaningfulness of doubting or suspending judgment. Spinoza started his system at the point that others were trying to attain after they overcame the skeptical menace. Spinoza eliminated the skeptics by first propounding the axiom "A true idea *must* correspond with that of which it is the idea" and later insisting that people have true ideas.[103] The evidence for the latter claim is personal experience; for the former, nothing except that it is an axiom. As an axiom it obviates the need to build bridges from ideas to objects. For Spinoza, there are no real skeptics, only ignoramuses.

Spinoza, at this point, set forth a brief picture of what human knowledge amounts to. It is interesting that most of the early modern philosophers made the theory of knowledge the heart of their philosophies. They engaged in what John Locke called "enquiry concerning the origins, extent, and certainty of our ideas." Spinoza leaves this until the end of Part 2, having already by then sketched out the kind of knowledge we can have of the physical and mental world. His brief epistemological discussion sets forth three kinds of knowledge that human beings can have. The first is knowledge from experience. This is what most people have. They do not understand it but they are able to use it and operate according to it. They not only have the bare experiences but also they learn rules of how to manipulate these experiences, how to combine them, and how to draw conclusions from them.

The second type of knowledge is rational knowledge, which involves understanding the concepts involved in making sense of our experience. These concepts can be purely mathematical ones.

The clearer our conceptual knowledge becomes the less possibility there is that there can be any error or doubt.

These two kinds of knowledge, empirical and rational, are what constitute the epistemological world of most seventeenth-century thinkers. Spinoza adds some suggestions at this point that there is another kind of knowledge. This knowledge of a third kind, intuitive knowledge, is more important and harder to achieve. As we shall see, this is the culmination of the human quest for understanding that is only reached at the end of one's philosophical journey, the intellectual love of God.

Spinoza then develops an account of how collections of modes constituting organisms persist in time. Descartes had portrayed everything in the world as being either a form of extension or a form of thought. The extended beings, which for Descartes are the entire mineral and animal kingdom, have no intellectual component. They survive only if not interfered with or destroyed by outside forces. Descartes and some of the Cartesians went so far as regarding animals as some kind of intricate machinery with no feeling whatsoever. The Cartesian view became harder and harder to accept the more the behavior of living organisms, plants, and animals was studied. Their responses to outside stimuli suggested some sort of feeling was involved plus some sort of attempt to persevere in spite of negative external influences. Spinoza, contrary to Descartes, sees the modal complex that constitutes a being as both physical and mental. It has a form that derives from its place in the divine order and endeavors to persevere in this form as long as possible. This endeavor he calls *conatus*. The self-preserving being can be affected by external forces and, hence, can be transformed or destroyed due to outside influence. Internally, the *conatus* will keep it striving for self-preservation as much as possible, carrying on the modal nature derived from the nature of God. *Conatus* will keep groups of modes in interaction and harmony as long as possible.

Spinoza, in Book three, then turns to examining and explaining the activities of sentient living creatures who are motivated by emotions. Emotive causality in terms of pain, suffering, and enjoyment, offer a way to explain how living beings move in various directions and toward various goals. As this explanatory system moves further and further up the scale of living beings, it becomes an all-encompassing explanation of human behavior.

Book four of the *Ethics* is entitled "Of Human Bondage." Here, Spinoza seeks to show to what extent human actions and decisions are caused by the emotional structure of human existence. In Spinoza's world everything is determined and cannot be otherwise. It would seem, therefore, that human beings have no choice as to how they behave. The struggle for Spinoza is not to break the causal chain that determines human behavior, but to change the evaluation of what human beings do. The first stage in this is understanding, developing a science of human activity. The more one knows about human psychology and about the physical causes of emotions, the more one realizes what is going on. Realizing this does not enable one to change but to overcome one's dependence on the physical structure of human life. Spinoza presents a basically Stoic worldview about human behavior. Everything is the way it is and cannot be changed but, on learning this, a human being can have a different attitude toward the state of affairs.

In a deterministic system there is always a difficulty in explaining how innovation can take place. For Spinoza the problem is, does the realization of the forces involved in human behavior become a cause of a change? Or does the human being, on understanding, introduce a new unproduced causal chain? If the latter, this would obviously break down the fully deterministic system. If the former, then is the change resulting from the force of understanding just another caused event that cannot be other than it is?

Spinoza, like the Stoics, seems to want to have it both ways. All human action is the result of prior causes. At the same time, some kinds of human action, like understanding, trigger off a new causal chain. Then the question is, what causes this new kind of action? In Spinoza's theory, people experience events and make rules about them for their self-preservation. If they go beyond this and try to understand what is going on then they reach the second kind of knowledge, understanding, and they are then part of another causal sequence. But why should one start inquiring into causes? Is it determined that some people will be inquirers and other people not? If so, then there is no reason for Spinoza's exhortations, trying to get people to understand their situation. They are either caused to become inquirers or they are caused to just accept events.

It is not only the Stoics and Spinoza who have a problem here. The ancient atomists seem to get into the same difficulty. In the original atomic theory of Democritus all events are due to the collision of atoms. The atoms are falling downward. Some of the collisions lead to atoms being knocked into another direction, colliding with still other atoms. In this initial atomic theory everything is necessary and if one knew the location and speed of each atom one could predict the whole future cause of history. Epicurus found this sort of total determinism too restrictive and introduced a modification, namely, that atoms could inexplicably go off in other directions uncaused. The gentle swerve would make the future unpredictable and every-thing could be said to be the result of the "fortuitous concourse of atoms." However, Epicurus's theory was supposed to relieve people from their anxieties about future events. If they under-stood that the future is indeterminate this would involve some volition on the part of the person seeking to understand and, we can ask, what might cause that?

In both Spinoza's case and that of the Stoics there is a knotty problem of whether human initiative is possible. If it is not, then there is no reason to urge people to get beyond their bondage and become free people. Those who are going to be free will be forced to be free by the causal process. An example of this shows clearly what the problem is. Some years ago I was at a conference dealing with Spinoza at which an eminent philosopher was espousing the problem of determinism in Spinoza. He was smoking a cigarette and coughing violently. As he was urging people to try and understand what was happening in their lives and thereby improve their lives, I suggested that if he really believed this he might ask himself why he was still smoking. Presumably, a spinozist would have realized a causal connection between the smoking and the coughing and would have tried to change the causal process. If the change was possible then what causes the change? Is it genuine initiative, or is it another kind of cause that we have not recognized yet, possibly some subconscious cause?

There have been many who question whether Spinoza's explanation is compatible with people changing their outlook or attitudes. How anybody perceives events, or understands them, is presumably part of the causal chain of human activities. One could go so far as to suggest that even trying to understand events is not a free option but the result of some sort of prior causal chain. Spinoza wants both to keep to a totally deterministic picture of human activity and, at the same time, to allow for some innovation in terms of human understanding. Many books and articles have been written on whether Spinoza can consistently have it both ways.

At the lowest level of human behavior, one acts because one has to and cannot do otherwise. If one begins to inquire about the cause of events one begins to understand the causal nexus that leads to the state of affairs one is living in. This in itself does not change anything but is, in fact, the way one passes from a state of being in bondage to the emotions to being a free human agent. The understanding of human events begins with a realization of the psychological mechanisms that control human behavior. If one seeks to comprehend what is involved, one starts the journey into the third kind of knowledge and human liberation. The third kind of knowledge, which Spinoza has only talked of sketchily before this, is an intuitive grasp of the larger and largest picture of what is going on, ultimately seeing the world from the aspect of eternity. In this state, one no longer sees one event following another but sees the whole panorama of events not as a sequence, but as a way God or Substance is modified.

The fifth book of the *Ethics* is entitled "Of Human Freedom." One of the more perplexing parts of Spinoza's account here is his use of the notion of human freedom. We are accustomed to thinking of freedom involving lack of constraint. For Spinoza, such a state of affairs is not good or desirable since the unrestrained person can make up an enormous range of possible actions, some desirable, some not. Real freedom in Spinoza's sense is freedom from the possibility of erroneous action or behavior, that is, a really free human being would be completely determined to do or think the right thing. A really free human being would be free because his or her actions were determined by higher causes. Whether such a person was still being controlled by other forces would no longer matter.

A person becomes free first by understanding as fully as possible what causes human beings to behave as they do. The understanding may in some cases lead to an adoption of the different causal nexus as in the case of people who stop smoking because of rational considerations. The person presumably first understands what it is that has produced the craving for nicotine, further realizes that nicotine is an addictive substance, and still further realizes that addiction can be overcome by various physical and psychological activities. If one can then gear one's life to being caused by these anti-smoking activities, a change in behavior is possible. But this does not prove that human beings have any freedom and self-determination but through rational effort can alter the deterministic path.

One can realize that some bodily functions, like breathing, urination, and ingestion, are ways in which the human organism keeps on functioning. These are ways in which one has very limited control. In contrast, there are other bodily developments that one can control to a great degree, like length of hair, bodily covering, type of diet, and so on. Presumably, the rational person will understand what the effects of various alterations in these activities would lead to. Spinoza is supposed to have lived on a very limited diet, sufficient to keep him alive but without much gourmet variety. He could have broadened his intake of food, realizing what this might do to other bodily functions and psychic attitudes, but he could not have decided not to eat and still remain in existence.

The picture of the free human being in Book five is a human being who understands the causal combinations which enable us to continue to function. Beyond this, Spinoza opens up the possibility not only of understanding human existence as it is, but also, as he terms it, "seeing the world from the aspect of eternity." If we not only see the world from the human perspective but also can get beyond this we can gain a higher form of knowledge. This is what he had hinted at earlier as intuitive knowledge that goes beyond the empirical and the rational. This sort of cosmic detachment leads to the final propositions of the *Ethics*.

Through the third kind of knowledge one reaches the intellectual love of God (*amor Dei intellectualis*). This becomes for Spinoza the only form of human immortality and of human blessedness. The *Ethics* reaches its ethical conclusion after ploughing through a great deal of metaphysics and science to rise to a kind of rational mysticism. Spinoza, at the very end, comments on his own success in gaining this end point by saying that "All things excellent are as difficult as they are rare."[104] Spinoza might have been extremely happy with his achievement. However, his one-time student Albert Burgh, who had forsaken Spinoza's philosophy for that of the Roman Catholic Church, raised some skeptical problems.

You claim to have discovered the true philosophy. How do you know that your philosophy is the best out of all those that have ever been taught in this world, are at present being taught, or will ever be taught in the future? To say nothing of possible future philosophies, have you examined all those philosophies throughout the entire world? And even if you have examined them properly, how do you know that you have chosen the best? You will say, my philosophy is in agreement with right reason, while the rest are opposed to it. But all other philosophers except for your followers disagree with you, and with the same right they claim for themselves and their philosophy exactly what you claim for yours, and accuse you of falsity and error just as you do them.[105]

Burgh showed some philosophical caution and raised a question that any philosopher has to face about his own theory – can you really be sure it is true? Spinoza, without hesitation, just brushed this aside with the announcement that he never said his was the best theory; he said it was *the* true theory.[106] He knows this just as he knows that the three angles of a triangle add up to two right angles; "that this suffices no one will deny who has a sound brain and does not dream of unclean spirits who inspire us with false ideas as if they were true. For truth reveals both itself and the false."[107]

Presumably, the extraordinary human effort that it takes to prove all the propositions in the five books of the *Ethics* has its own reward in terms of finding the ultimate good for a human being. The conception of the intellectual love of God as the ultimate achievement a human being can reach is from the sixteenth-century Jewish poet and philosopher Leone Ebreo. Leone Ebreo was a leading Renaissance Neo-Platonist and kabbalist following the theories of Marcilio Ficino and Solomon ibn Gabirol. His major philosophical work, *Dialoghi d'Amore*, contains the idea of the intellectual love of God. A copy of this work in Spanish was found in Spinoza's small library and probably influenced its owner.

Because the printing distribution of the *Tractatus* had been so successful, the guardians of public morality worried about any further work of Spinoza that might appear. Spinoza had informed enough people over the years that he was writing the major statement of his philosophy. By 1675, when he had completed the *Ethics*, people in England, France, Germany, and the Netherlands heard rumors about this. When Spinoza approached his publisher about delivering a manuscript, he was warned about the all-out efforts that would ensue to suppress the work. De Witt's liberal government was now gone and its replacement was bringing back more and more restrictions. Spinoza was warned that a great outcry would occur if the *Ethics* appeared in print, greater even than that which the *Tractatus* had produced. He decided to set it aside and made arrangements to ensure it would appear shortly after his death. His own health problems had probably made him aware that he would not live much longer, so the focus was on making arrangements for the posthumous publication and to avoid any censorship before publication took place.

Was Spinoza afraid of censorship or persecution? He knew from the time he was still in the synagogue that his ideas were not approved of. Should he have been wary from then on? It was just before Spinoza's excommunication that Isaac La Peyrère had been arrested for what he had written in the *Prae-Adamitae*. Since the book had come out in Amsterdam in five editions and Spinoza used it liberally, he would probably have known the story of what happened to Isaac La Peyrère.

Although the Netherlands was renowned for its tolerance there were occasional points at which the society felt somebody had gone too far. Spinoza himself never seems to have been in clear and present danger but friends of his, such as Adriaan Koerbagh and his brother, did get arrested and charged with blasphemy. Adriaan died in jail after being severely punished. Before Koerbagh, Spinoza's Latin teacher Franciscus Van den Enden had been forbidden to teach by the Dutch authorities in 1662. He ultimately ended up being executed by the French authorities in 1674 for trying to overthrow the French monarchy and create a democratic republic. Spinoza's friend Lodewijk Meyer had been very careful in spelling out his own evaluation of biblical themes in philosophical terms in order to avoid condemnation. Spinoza himself was involved in some sort of defensive subterfuge in planning how the *Tractatus* would appear by having it published with a false title page indicating it was printed in Germany. Dutch censorship laws applied to books published in the Netherlands and not to foreign volumes. Spinoza also had published the *Tractatus* in Latin so he could not be accused of inciting the masses or the ignorant and, as mentioned earlier, he begins and ends the *Tractatus* with the statement that if the civil authorities decide there is anything wrong with the book he will gladly make the changes requested. There is no evidence, however, that any changes were suggested or that he entertained any, and the text remained as he wrote it. Spinoza never wrote anything further defending the text but added some notes to chapter 6 that indicate the Cartesian basis of some of his ideas. These precautions do indicate that he realized some of the dangers involved in publishing his work. The discussion about what he said to others about his book, however, would indicate that he was not hiding his views at all. He was not, as Yirmiahu Yovel said, a *marrano* of reason, hiding his rationalism.[108] Instead, we are told by Colonel Stouppe and Minister Le Brun that he was quite specific about his thoroughgoing rationalism.

Leo Strauss, in his book *Persecution and the Art of Writing*, portrays Maimonides, Hobbes, and Spinoza as prime examples of people responding to the fear of persecution. According to Strauss, the alert and intelligent reader would learn how to read between the lines and to read what was not said as well as what was said.[109] I do not think this truly applies in Spinoza's case since he was very explicit about his criticism of the Bible, biblical interpretation, and the value of religious teachings. He apparently knew how far he could go and still die of old age or consumption. The fact that he did not press ahead with the publication of the *Ethics* indicates that he knew when the authorities would step in. One has to fit all this in with the fact that there was only a small amount of censorship in the Netherlands in the seventeenth century but it could be very severe. Authors and publishers knew how to get around some of the difficulties, such as using false title pages, hiding the books when the police came, and so on. Similarly, interested readers knew how to get hold of the books.

Jonathan Israel describes the secretive and furious-paced gathering of the text for the *Opera Posthuma*, which was to include the *Ethics*, selections from his correspondence, and smaller pieces.[110] These were to be published simultaneously in the Latin original and in Dutch. It also appeared shortly thereafter in French with false title pages. Considering how radical Spinoza's views about religion and its role in society were, it is surprising that there was no immediate reaction to the work and no refutations for several years.

Later life and posthumous influence

Spinoza received visits in The Hague from intellectuals from all over Europe. According to his landlord, people would come to see him in the late morning and afternoon to discuss intellectual concerns. The landlord also mentioned that Spinoza did not always exclude Jews from these discussions. We know at least two people of Jewish background who knew Spinoza in the 1670s. One of them is Henri Morelli, an Egyptian Jew who was a medical doctor to aristocratic patients. Morelli indicated that he and Spinoza talked at length about Spinoza's affairs. The other identifiable Jewish person is Gabriel Milan, a wealthy Jewish merchant from Copenhagen who was the son-in-law of the chief rabbi there. Milan was a business agent for the king of Denmark in The Hague and was present with Spinoza to give testimony in support of a Dutch army officer at the time of Condé's invasion.[111] So, he seems to have been in contact with some members of the Jewish community towards the end of his life.

According to the biography of Spinoza written by Colerus, among Spinoza's effects there were over two hundred charcoal drawings made by Spinoza of people who had come to call on him, including some "ladies of quality." Colerus, writing in the early eighteenth century, describes holding these drawings in his hands so they still existed more than twenty-five years after the philosopher's death. If they could be found we would have a much richer picture of Spinoza's social life. Also, if we knew about his associations we would have a fuller picture of Spinoza's late adult life and would be able to see him not as a lonely, ostracized truth-seeker but as an intellectual sought after by many of his contemporaries.

Leibniz, like many other learned people of the time, began to hear about Spinoza as an expert in optics and other subjects and initiated a correspondence in 1671. They arranged ways in which they could exchange further letters. Leibniz was interested enough in Spinoza to discuss anecdotes about the philosopher with Spinoza's last landlord Van der Spyck. Leibniz also learned from his teacher Thomasius about Spinoza's irreligious views, Thomasius being one of the first to refute Spinoza on this score. Later on, Leibniz claimed he had never read Spinoza's work on this subject but just a few years ago Leibniz's own copy of the *Tractatus* was located by Ursula Goldenbaum. Leibniz had written all over his copy, showing his disapproval in many places. Leibniz went to England in 1673 and was inducted into the Royal Society there. Among the people he came into contact with was Sir Henry Oldenburg, Spinoza's friend for many years. Oldenburg tried to use Leibniz as a mail courier and the last letter Oldenburg wrote to Spinoza was sent via Leibniz. We know that the letter was never delivered. Oldenburg was very upset and tried to find out why Leibniz did not deliver the letter. As yet, no sign of the document has been uncovered in the Leibniz archives or elsewhere.

As Spinoza became more notorious, and denounced everywhere for his philosophical views, Leibniz tried to minimize his interest in Spinoza's ideas. However, he did try to find out about Spinoza's unpublished manuscript, the *Ethics*, when he was in Paris in 1672. He went to see the scientist and mathematician Walther Ehrenfried von Tschirnhaus who knew Spinoza and was in correspondence with him. Tschirnhaus had a manuscript copy of the *Ethics* and had promised his friend Spinoza that he would not show it to anybody without his permission. When Leibniz pressed Tschirnhaus to let him peek at it Tschirnhaus asked Spinoza for permission, which was denied. Spinoza did not grant permission because he was worried about what Leibniz was up to. Specifically, he was concerned about why Leibniz was in the French capital at the very time that the Netherlands had been captured by the French army under the prince of Condé. Leibniz was a diplomat and involved in meeting foreign officials wherever he went. So, Spinoza may have had some reason to be cautious in case the ideas in his manuscript became known to the wrong people. However, despite Tchirnhaus's refusal to let him see the manuscript, Leibniz did gain some idea as to what was in Spinoza's great book from his conversations with Tchirnhaus and there are notes by Leibniz about what he learned of the content of Spinoza's metaphysics.[112]

Spinoza was somewhat attracted by the possibility of having a career outside of the Netherlands. Following on this was an account that was to be of great significance in the Spinoza literature: the rumor that the prince of Condé tried to get Spinoza to become his court philosopher. The French had invaded the Netherlands in 1672 and the country was effectively destroyed for a while as the dykes were opened to stop the invasion. Up until World War II, this invasion remained the worst horror in Dutch history: the prince of Condé was remembered as one of the greatest villains, so an invitation from him was not a matter to be taken lightly. One of the most important figures on the European scene wanted to meet Spinoza.

Because of Condé's reputation in the Netherlands, the possibility of Spinoza having met the prince has remained a troublesome item. Spinoza was invited to the prince's headquarters in Utrecht. He went and returned to The Hague with lots of presents from the prince but insisted he had not met him. Some of those in the entourage of the prince, however, insisted for years after that Spinoza and the prince did talk day after day, that the prince made Spinoza a fine offer to come to Paris, but that Spinoza decided that, as powerful as the prince of Condé may have been, he could not protect him from the hostility of the bigoted religious authorities in France. It is interesting at this point to recall that the secretary of the prince of Condé in the middle of the1650s was Isaac La Peyrère, the author of the *Prae-Adamitae* and *Du Rappel des Juifs*. La Peyrère, in the 1650s, was in contact with Menasseh ben Israel in Amsterdam and could easily have met Spinoza then. The prince of Condé might have heard something about Spinoza from his former secretary who had since retired to an Oratorian monastery in Paris.

What seems to be agreed upon is that Spinoza was invited by the prince to come and visit him in Utrecht and that Spinoza made a voyage under very difficult conditions to get there. One of the prince's top officers, Colonel J.-B. Stouppe, made the arrangements and accompanied Spinoza from The Hague to Utrecht.[113]

Condé was not just a general; he was also a great patron of arts and literature. His home in Paris was an intellectual center for Descartes, Pascal, Gassendi, Mersenne, and many others who met and discussed new discoveries. Condé was also a patron of the leading playwrights Corneille, Racine and Molière. The Condé papers, which are housed at his former chateau at Chantilly, have not yet yielded anything definitive about the Spinoza visit. There are mentions by some of Condé's entourage of expecting him. There is an item where Stouppe's brother explains to Condé, who is then back in Paris, that Spinoza had come by and reminds the prince who Spinoza was. There are connections between some of the people in Condé's entourage and Spinoza, including Saint-Glain, the translator of the *Tractatus* into French. Some others are supposed to have been in the group that stayed on in the Netherlands after the French army was withdrawn. It is members of this group who were involved in what is called the earliest biography of Spinoza attributed to Jean-Maximilien Lucas.[114]

It is interesting that not only Spinoza and his friends but also Stouppe tried to distance himself from the stories about the meeting. Stouppe, in 1672, was writing a book called *La Religion des Hollandois*, which was a kind of justification of Condé's invasion of Holland. According to Stouppe, the Netherlands was making no effort to keep law and order and even, also according to Stouppe, allowed a complete non-believer, Spinoza, to function. Stouppe then cites little bits of the *Tractatus* as evidence. This is one of the first mentions of Spinoza in the context of the intellectual activity of the time. Stouppe was apparently writing this, according to the dates in his publication, at the very time he was arranging Spinoza's visit to Condé.[115]

It is also interesting that a biography of the prince of Condé by Pierre Coste (John Locke's French secretary and a close friend of Pierre Bayle), translated into English in 1693, states bluntly that Condé

> Was desirous to see Spinoza and told him smiling, that if he would follow him into France, he would put him in a way to live conforming to the Principles of his Theology; that Paris neither wanted fine Women, nor Pleasures; although he look'd upon him as a Deist, and a Man who had no Religion, he was charm'd with the Conversation he had with him.[116]

A further indication that there is more to the Spinoza/Condé story than was reported by Spinoza, and has come down to us in the early biographies, is the account given by a friend of Spinoza's at the time, Henri Morelli. From an interview in London between the journalist Pierre Desmaizeaux and Morelli, which is recounted in the notes to one of Pierre Bayle's letters, Desmaizeaux reported the following statement by Morelli:

> I have known very particularly Mr. Spinoza. He has spoken to me more than one time of having been at Utrecht with the prince of Conde, the prince after talking with him, wanted him to follow him to Paris, and remain there as part of his entourage; in addition he could count on his protection, he would house and

feed him, and give him a thousand écus as a pension: to which Spinoza responded, that he thanked his highness in considering him but that he did not think that his power was capable of protecting him from the bigotry of the court around which his name was already strongly denounced because of the Tractatus Theologico-Politicus.[117]

Morelli, who had studied medicine in Italy and the Netherlands, was the doctor to Ninon de Lenclos, the famous Parisian courtesan, and to the countess of Southampton, the daughter of the libertine earl of Rochester.[118] In the mid 1670s Morelli was living in England functioning as Saint-Évremond's doctor. He was also involved with John Dryden, who thanked Morelli for his help in studying the Italian version of Virgil's *Aeneid*. Morelli became a member of the college of physicians and surgeons, was a contact for Sir Hans Sloane of the English Royal Society with Dutch medical societies, and was a friend of the radical Irish deist John Toland. It would be interesting to know if Morelli and Spinoza discussed anything about their common Sephardic backgrounds. Morelli, when he moved to England, presented himself as a Catholic and appears on some records as belonging to Catholic parishes. In the Netherlands he does not seem to have any clear religious affiliation. Saint-Évremond treats him as a completely free spirit and his comments indicate that Morelli had rather avant-garde opinions about religion that seem to be like those of Spinoza.[119]

Pierre Bayle and Pierre Desmaizeaux were both very suspicious of the story about Spinoza's relations with the prince of Condé. Bayle had heard from a young Dutch bookseller and printer Francis Halma that he, Halma, had seen Spinoza going into the prince's quarters day after day. Halma had a bookstore across the street from the papal palace that the prince was using as his headquarters. Desmaizeaux followed through on Bayle's suspicions and interviewed a French refugee in England who had been one of Condé's surgeons, who also confirmed Spinoza's visits plus telling of the conversations that Condé and Spinoza had exchanged.

It is curious that Spinoza scholars have not followed up on the Bayle/Desmaizeaux accounts, especially since they are also supported by the text of the *Life of Condé* published in England at the time by Pierre Coste and by what the duc d'Aumale reported finding in the Condé archives, which he had inherited. At any rate, either in the Bayle/Desmaizeaux version or the usual one coming from Colerus and Lucas, Spinoza did spend quite a bit of time with the Condé entourage.

When Spinoza returned from his trip to Utrecht he found that an angry mob had killed the prime minister, Jan de Witt, and dismembered his body. Spinoza later told Leibniz in their one and only meeting that he made a placard in Latin saying, "This is the Ultimate in Barbarism" and was prepared to march into the throng of people. According to Spinoza's story, his landlord, Hendrik van der Spyck, had to physically restrain him to prevent him from becoming one more victim to the tragedy of that day.

In 1673, Spinoza had another opportunity to leave the Netherlands when he was approached about taking up a professorship at the University of Heidelberg. Some of the details of this are a bit foggy. Spinoza wrote an impassioned defense of freedom of thought in turning down the offer. He said that he did not want to be responsible for the closure of the university and he did not want to be restricted in any way as to what he could say or teach. However, Pierre Bayle claimed at the outset that he had heard a quite different version of Spinoza's involvement with the authorities at Heidelberg. Bayle's information indicated that Spinoza only wrote his remarkable rejection of a position at the great university *after* they had withdrawn the offer. Bayle apparently got his information from a visiting diplomat from the Palatine, whereby the authorities of Heidelberg apparently had second thoughts, worried about Spinoza's radical views, and had already withdrawn the offer before Spinoza's refusal.[120] Thereafter, Spinoza seems to have resigned himself to living out his years in the Netherlands. It is possible that he had used up the options he had for leaving the country and thus foresaw that he would spend the rest of his days in the Netherlands.

In the literature about Spinoza, three events are made decisive in explaining his character. First, his refusal to accept the offer of the synagogue to stay with them and just appear once a year for the High Holidays and to keep quiet; second, his refusal of the post at Heidelberg; and, third, his refusal to meet with the prince of Condé. The first shows that Spinoza was not a hypocrite, the second that he put the search for truth above all else, and the third, that he was not interested in political patronage no matter where it came from. For over 300 years there has been a sustained effort to keep up the image that these events indicate. As noted above, there is much doubt about each one of the episodes. However, one could expect that not everything he did was completely free from blemish and, regardless, he still stands out as a much more interesting and moral character than any other philosopher of modern times.

In 1677 Spinoza developed consumption and died at the young age of forty-four. He was buried in the cemetery of the New Church in The Hague. A couple of months later, Spinoza's complete works (minus the *Tractatus*) was published in Amsterdam. This included the *Ethics* and several of the unfinished works. Spinoza was now launched on the intellectual world with the complete text of his major work. This edition also included eighty-three letters selected by his friends and students as being the most philosophical. It seems that a rather severe housecleaning had taken place. Spinoza, from what we know about his life, was in contact with an increasingly wide group of people in the Netherlands and some in other countries and his interests were fairly extensive in terms of philosophy, science, and politics. Those who edited his literary remains seem to have removed most of this material. There is no sign or mention of de Witt in the papers that survive nor the relationship between Spinoza and Charles Saint-Évremond, for example, even though Spinoza was supposed to have been quite friendly with him and they apparently met from time to time and talked of many things. On the other hand, one document found in recent years gives a very negative picture of what Spinoza was like. Bishop Pierre-Daniel Huet of Avranches and Spinoza knew quite a few people in common, including Tschirnhaus and Leibniz, but they never met in person or corresponded. When Huet learned of Spinoza's death, he wrote his friend Étienne Le Moine, a Protestant preacher in Leiden who knew Spinoza personally, and asked the man for details about Spinoza's character. Instead of the almost saintly picture that we have received from other sources Le Moine said of Spinoza that he had:

> ... a bad countenance, and the physiognomy promises only that which is base and contemptible. His mind was comprised of Judaism, Socinianism, and of libertinism, and if he had lived in Constantinople, Peking, or Tokyo, he would just as gladly have entered into Mohammadism, Taoism, or Buddhism.[121]

We do not know whether Le Moine's description agreed with that of others who knew Spinoza but it does indicate there was another side to the story as to how he was regarded by his contemporaries. The hagiographic image that has been handed down to us may at least partially result from the destruction of so much of his correspondence. In addition, such a picture was given in the earlier biography of Spinoza by Lucas and, except for this one comment, this side of Spinoza is also not evident at all in the material we have. In fact, there are just two pieces of correspondence in the preserved material that could suggest this other, less saintly, Spinoza. These are the letters to Hugo Boxel and to Albert Burgh. Boxel had told Spinoza that he believed in ghosts and spirits. Spinoza treats his views with contempt and does not want to be bothered with discussing this anymore with him. Burgh, who had become an important convert to Catholicism, tried to bring his mentor to his new religious life. In replying to his former student, Spinoza's text is quite angry. So there are slight indications that make Spinoza more human than the portrayal presented by Bayle, Colerus and Lucas.[122]

Although it is sometimes said that Spinoza was only taken seriously about a century after his writing, he was being discussed as he was publishing his first works and when his posthumous writings appeared in 1677. One finds discussions, excerpts, and partial refutations of portions of his text among a wide range of writers in the first half of the eighteenth century.[123]

Bayle was concerned to show Spinoza's strength, that he was the first to make atheism into a system, that he was a completely moral person, and that his philosophy was a mass of confusion and contradictions. Spinoza's philosophy, according to Bayle, is close to that of Confucianism. The writings of Confucius had just appeared in French and European awareness of the rich treasures of Chinese thought was just beginning. Bayle, from a sampling of this, mentioned that he saw some similarity between Spinoza's thought and that of the Chinese. This note keeps being brought up even in present day discussions that there seems to be some congruence between Spinoza's pantheism and the spiritual metaphysics of Buddhism.

For Bayle, the fact that Spinoza had created a system of atheism was very significant. Throughout the *Dictionnaire* Bayle had been poking holes in all sorts of theologies and philosophies, showing that they were all "big with contradiction and absurdity." In contrast, Bayle's Spinoza had created a system of atheism and this intellectual triumph was coupled with Spinoza's moral character.

Bayle was an expert at describing and criticizing philosophical and theological theories. He had analyzed theories from ancient times up to the latest theories of Malebranche and Leibniz, and was able to see the logical structure of each theory and then exhibit the faults to be found in each theory. The *Dictionnaire* is a monument to the dialectical skills of Bayle. The one article in which this seems to fall apart is that of Spinoza. Each time, in this long article in which Bayle attempts to describe Spinoza's view, he quickly becomes incoherent. This happened so much that people told Bayle that he did not understand Spinoza's theory and that he should get somebody to explain it to him. In the second edition of the *Dictionnaire* in 1702, Bayle describes sitting down with a disciple of Spinoza and going over the text of the *Ethics* line by line. Then, when Bayle came to explicate it, the same thing happened – Spinoza's theory became incoherent. This is, in fact, Bayle's criticism, that there is no way of stating atheism coherently. He uses his dialectical skill to demonstrate this over and over again.

As new critiques of Spinoza's theory began circulating in France, the Netherlands, Germany, and England readers found more congenial ways of attacking Spinoza's worldview than the long presentation in Bayle. Bayle's critique became less and less relevant so that even though Bayle's article on Spinoza was one of the most widely read statements about Spinoza in the eighteenth century, it had less and less influence as criticism of Spinoza's thought.

In Bayle's text, he mentions a contemporary Dutch thinker Johannes Bredenbourg who set out to refute Spinoza line by line. He ended up establishing exactly the same theory as Spinoza, which he then said he rejected and on the basis of faith preserved his anti-spinozistic stance. Bredenbourg was a friend of Isaac Orobio de Castro, who wrote the only critique of Spinoza that has come down to us by a member of the Jewish community of Amsterdam. Orobio's criticism was considered one of the best and it is included in a collection of critiques that was edited by the French bishop François Fénelon.[124] Fénelon's secretary, the Chevalier Andrew Michael Ramsay, offered a detailed meta-physical refutation of Spinoza. Ramsay was a leading Scottish convert to Catholicism. In the 1720s and 1730s he became the leader of the freemasons in France and was the teacher of Bonny Prince Charlie. Ramsay took Spinoza very seriously and went into careful detail about problems in Spinoza's definitions in the beginning of Book one of the *Ethics*. He showed how, if one altered the definitions, one would not end up with what he kept referring to as the monstrous consequences of Spinoza's system. He also argued that George Berkeley presented a better answer to Spinoza than did Leibniz, though both failed to provide a satisfactory answer to Spinoza's metaphysical threat. Ramsay's critique of Spinoza has been overlooked because it only appeared in a posthumous work, *The Philosophical Principles of Natural and Revealed Religion*, a volume which does not appear to have been taken seriously in the mid-eighteenth century. However, Ramsay was also the patron of a young Scottish scholar David Hume who came to France in 1734 to write his first book, *A Treatise of Human Nature*. Ramsay thought Hume was going to be a great metaphysician but when he saw a draft of Hume's *Treatise* he realized that Hume was going off in other directions. Nonetheless, in a section of the *Treatise* that gets very little attention, Hume follows on Ramsay's critique of Spinoza and discusses in great detail what he saw as fundamental problems in the spinozistic theory.[125] Ramsay had tried to show that there could be two kinds of substances, one infinite and the other finite, and that this would not lead to the spinozistic conclusions that only one substance can exist. Hume seems to be building on some of Ramsay's points. It may seem strange that Ramsay, who ended up a mystic, and Hume, a skeptic, should come together in their metaphysical critique of Spinoza. Ramsay is supposed to have had a serious impact in American philosophy especially through Jonathan Edwards, so there may be further developments that came from his theory.[126]

Spinoza's discussion of freedom of speech and discussion and the role of this in the modern state has been overshadowed by those of John Locke and Pierre Bayle. Spinoza had offered the most careful presentation of the need for unfettered discussion as a condition of a modern society. Locke, whose views dominated the discussion of the time, had tried to limit freedom of expression in cases where the state or church might feel threatened. Locke was quite upset when he was accused of being a spinozist by one William Carroll, who said that Locke's view that it is possible that mental substance can be extended and physical substance can think would lead to atheism. Locke had claimed that we just do not know enough to rule out these possibilities. Carroll pounced on this and insisted that Locke was really upholding Spinoza's pantheism in which mind and matter were the same substance. Locke was very upset by this attack and fought back vigorously. Pierre Bayle tempered his own views on freedom of expression because he started worrying about possible effects of unlimited expression by people who wanted to do harm to others. Spinoza, in theory, expressed the broadest claims to freedom of expression offered at the time while at the same time withdrawing them if they threatened the state. On the second theme, Spinoza was willing to allow the state to do whatever was necessary to safeguard the well being of its citizens.

One of the most influential parts of Spinoza's view was that concerning his way of interpreting the Bible and, in the years after Spinoza, his critique of religion was taken up by radicals in the early French Enlightenment. The *Tractatus* appeared in French in 1671 with three different false titles. The translator is believed to have been someone from the prince of Condé's entourage, Saint-Glain. This brought about a much greater dispersion of Spinoza's ideas, which became very widespread in the French-speaking world where they were used to criticize the philosophy of the *ancien régime* and the Catholic Church, and to point the way to a new free era of thought. There had been a current amongst some aristocratic writers and thinkers that was critical of the religious structures and beliefs of the time. From the Renaissance onward one finds indications of freethinking amongst a wide variety of intellectuals. This made them open to new kinds of ideas that might support some of their critiques of existing religion. It has also been shown by Alan Kors in his book *Atheism in France* that, even in the theological institutes, they liked to try their skills at refuting or deflecting atheistic arguments.[127] Hence, there was a ripe field for spinozism to take root in France. In the very popular *Memoirs of a Turkish Spy Living in*

Paris by J. P. Marana, the Lost Tribes of Israel, who had just been found, are portrayed as excellent human beings who are vegetarians and spinozists.

One of the first people to deal in detail with Spinoza's ideas was the Comte Henri de Boulainvilliers who first wanted to become clear as to what Spinoza was advocating in order to answer him. Boulainvilliers felt that Bayle had not made a sufficient effort to understand Spinoza and, as a result, had made the refutation of him more difficult by his confused presentation. Boulainvilliers worked for a while just trying to get a carefully stated presentation of Spinoza's arguments. Then, when he set to work to refute this, he found that he was unable to. At first, he was going to join Bayle and others in advocating the fideistic approach, that one should admit that Spinoza cannot be answered rationally but by faith one can overcome his arguments. However, when he tried expounding this, he found that he was, in fact, convinced that Spinoza was right and worked out a clear presentation in French of his arguments. He did not publish this because of possible censorship and penal difficulties. His manuscript works circulated widely, despite being officially banned, and led others to see Spinoza as the one who was presenting them with the basis of an enlightened perspective beyond any religiously based philosophy. Prince Eugene of Savoy in his collections in Austria and The Hague had a copy of Boulainvilliers' manuscript. His ideas were taken up by others in France such as the Marquis D'Argenson, the *philosophe* Jean Lévesque de Burigny and the radical deist Nicolas Lenglet Dufresnoy.[128]

Bayle's article was widely read throughout the eighteenth century and provided a starting point for many Enlightenment figures to learn about Spinoza. Furthermore, the French version of the *Tractatus* was still being read a century later by people looking for arguments against organized religion. This led to Spinoza being appropriated both as a personality and as a secular thinker by Diderot, Voltaire, and others. Voltaire made the Bible into a very nasty picture of what human life was like a few millennia back. Within a hundred years of Spinoza, people like Tom Paine were saying that the Bible was just a compilation of lies, fables, and superstitions that no longer had any relevance. Paine, on being released from jail during the French Revolution, immediately requested a copy of the *Tractatus* and then cited something from the French edition in his work *Age of Reason*. Paine was especially attracted by Spinoza's biblical criticism. If Spinoza was right, then there was great doubt about whether Moses could be the author of the Pentateuch, or at least the entire Pentateuch, and as Paine said, if one denied the Mosaic authorship then all of the Old Testament falls. This became a major anti-religious usage of Spinoza that has been employed over the last two and a half centuries.[129]

Spinoza's ideas were banned and denounced all the time but they were also spread both in manuscript form and in books. The eighteenth century saw an immense increase in clandestine publication. Two works that appeared in the Netherlands, *La Vie de M. Spinoza* and *L'esprit de M. Spinoza*, contain the use of Spinoza's ideas to attack the religious establishment. The first work, attributed to Jean Maximilien Lucas, portrays Spinoza as a most saintly man beset by various bigoted adversaries. The second work, *L'esprit*, is also titled *Traité des Trois Imposteurs*, the three imposters being Moses, Jesus, and Mohammed. The work contains excerpts from Spinoza including his sharp attack on religious thinking in the appendix to Book one of the *Ethics*. It also contains material from Thomas Hobbes, La Mothe Le Vayer, and other avant-garde thinkers. *L'esprit* is basically a pastiche of texts with no original material. Almost all copies of the manuscript come with additional material, including discussions of Descartes and some late seventeenth-century authors. Hence, the work was probably put together in the last decade of the seventeenth century or the early part of the eighteenth. This work was printed in the Netherlands in 1719 but was immediately suppressed.[130] Nevertheless, it circulated widely in manuscript, almost always in the French text. Seventy-two manuscript copies of the printed copy were made and have been found in libraries all over the globe. A second printing occurred in the 1730s and thereafter other printing editions took place on into the twentieth century. There is even a printing at the end of the eighteenth century saying it was done under the auspices of George Washington, which is certainly not the case.

In England, radical deists were also discussing Spinoza around the turn of the century. His work was praised by Charles Blount who translated the chapter on miracles from the *Tractatus* and may also have been the author of the complete English translation of the *Tractatus* that appeared in 1689. As an interesting aside, the English translation of the *Tractatus* was reprinted in the middle of the eighteenth century. There is no indication of why it was done or who edited it. The volume may have played some part in the discussions about basic democratic principles that were taking place at the beginning of the American Revolution. A copy of the *Tractatus* in English was in the library of Benjamin Franklin and was used as a resource by those taking part in the constitutional debates of 1776. I have personally examined the copy from Franklin's library and unfortunately there are no markings and no indication as to who might have read it.

A much later sign of Spinoza's influence in England is the interest in him by the poet and essayist Samuel Taylor Coleridge. At the end of the eighteenth century Coleridge studied at the University of Göttingen and became aware of the new philosophical ideas coming out of the post-Kantian philosophers. When Coleridge returned to England and started writing about the new philosophical ideas emerging on the continent, he acknowledged the importance of Spinoza for the theories of the German Romantics. It is reported that he got in serious trouble with the English authorities when he and Robert Southey were apprehended when they were discussing Spy Nozi. It took quite a while to convince the police that this was quite a different kind of discussion, and not quite so dangerous.[131]

In Germany, in the latter part of the eighteenth century, Spinoza was a central figure in the discussions by Moses Mendelssohn and Gotthold Lessing. Spinoza had been denounced by many philosophical theologians in Germany. In spite of this, by the middle of the eighteenth century, Lessing was able to present a fresh look at Spinoza, seeing him as a harbinger of the Enlightenment philosophy that was spreading over Europe. He found that he was attracted to Spinoza's progressive ideas and began advocating some of them and supposedly revealed on his deathbed that he was actually a follower of Spinoza. Lessing's views led to what is called the *Atheismusstreit* and the *Pantheismusstreit* in which Spinoza was seen as the cause of modern atheism and pantheism; German philosophers fought over whether one could be an honest philosopher without being a spinozistic atheist. Lessing's close friend Moses Mendelssohn, who did not share Lessing's admiration for Spinoza's system, did, however, appreciate Spinoza's role as the first modern Jew to take part in general philosophical developments. Mendelssohn, who was called by his contemporaries the Jewish Socrates, indicated that within Judaism a new flowering of Enlightenment could occur if Jewish intellectuals would open themselves up to the new intellectual world. Mendelssohn did not advocate spinozism but did see Spinoza as an intellectual role model. The importance of Spinoza for Mendelssohn was that he raised the problem of whether Jewish or Christian philosophers could find any reasonable basis for their faith or whether they had to seek a faith outside of traditional religion.[132]

Some German thinkers exploring Spinoza's pantheistic notion of God began fusing it with the new metaphysical concepts of German idealism and transformed Spinoza from a villain to an actual hero whose ideas could play a most important role in their contemporary discussions. For some of the German philosophers in the last decade of the eighteenth century, Spinoza was seen as a "God intoxicated man" who could show them the way beyond the limits of traditional religion and traditional philosophy. Spinoza was now seen as a major figure in developing the modern outlook. A new edition of his works, the first since 1677, appeared. Writers such as Goethe and Herder happily pronounced themselves as spinozists. Fichte, Schelling, and Hegel all wrestled with Spinoza's theory and tried to show that their own new metaphysics took account of Spinoza's notion of substance and human freedom.

Spinoza, unlike most philosophers, has gained in stature as a personality and role model above and apart from his ideas and arguments. Most figures who are studied in the history of philosophy are known for their ideas rather than their personal contribution. What one knows about people like John Locke, Immanuel Kant, and others would not inspire any admiration. In Spinoza's case, from the end of his life in 1677 onward, he has been seen as the model of what an intellectual should be. Although the first criticisms of Spinoza always referred to his theory being hideous, monstrous, and vile, the man himself, from the time of Bayle's account, has been portrayed as an excellent human being. The picture of Spinoza as detached and usually imperturbable and thoughtful has put him above and beyond almost all philosophers in the last few centuries. What we know of figures like Descartes, Hume, Hegel, and Russell is not always commendable. In contrast, Spinoza seems to be portrayed as the ideal of what a dedicated intellectual can be. This image is probably the result of not having a great deal of his correspondence, which his students destroyed at the time of his death, and from the emphasis in Bayle, Lucas, and Colerus on his moral character. So, Spinoza as a teacher and as a person rises above the rest of the modern philosophers in this respect. People who have never read him still feel that he is one of philosophy's greatest heroes because of his model personality and the picture that is usually given of his trials and torments at the hands of religious zealots. I have recently been told by a philosopher, who had just passed through Holland as a tourist, that the most impressive sight he saw was Spinoza's little house with his lens-grinding machine and his small library. He spoke of this as a most inspiring place where one could feel the vibrations of modern philosophy.

In this volume I have tried to show that there is much more to the story of his life and hard times. Although we have fairly little definite information about Spinoza's life, by now we do know that he was not a poor, starving person making his living grinding lenses while thinking the most sublime thoughts. He was not isolated from the main currents of events of his time. We do not know enough to throw any more light on what his climatic difficulties were with the Amsterdam synagogue. Neither he nor his opponents have said enough to give us any real clues as to what happened in those early years. Also, we do not know much about his interaction with the Collegiants beyond the fact that he started drafting some of his philosophical statements while he was in their company. By the time Henry Oldenburg met him in 1661 he seems to have developed most of his philosophical system. We do not know exactly about the motivations that led him to publish the *Tractatus* and to take on the whole religious establishment. But Spinoza was aware of the persecutions of some of his friends for having made unacceptable remarks about religion. He was also aware of what happened to those in England who were not of the dominant group and he was living his own example of someone who was excommunicated. Why, at this particular time, he decided to mount a philosophical attack on religious orthodoxy we do not know. If we had more of his correspondence or accounts of him by people who met with him, he might turn out to be more of a flesh-and-blood character and not just an ideal figure. He has played an enormous and seminal role in the transformation of philosophy as the handmaiden of theology to philosophy as part of the emerging scientific world.

In the course of the nineteenth century, Spinoza became a prime object of serious study in terms of his life and history and thought. Many monographs were written on him and he has ever since been one of the seminal figures to be considered. During the last decades there has been a swell of new interest in Spinoza. New translations have been made in the United States, Europe, and Japan. Spinoza societies are springing up in many countries. One is about to emerge in Russia. There are specialized journals such as *Studia Spinoziana* to report on new findings about Spinoza, new interpretations, and new books. A Spinoza institute has been established in Jerusalem. Thus, he still remains one of the most seminal thinkers of the last four hundred years.

Spinoza showed practically no interest in his Jewish past. He lived his entire life in the Netherlands and does not seem to have been affected by anything concerning his Jewish background. He was occasionally called a Jew or his views were attributed to the fact that he was Jewish, but, aside from this, there does not seem to have been any active anti-Semitism in the world in which he functioned. Henry Méchoulan, in his interesting book *Être juif à Amsterdam au temps de Spinoza* (To Be a Jew in Amsterdam at the Time of Spinoza), expresses the fact that Spinoza's reaction to topics of interest to Jews was not in harmony with the Jewish community. The picture Méchoulan gives us is that essentially Spinoza was stone deaf to Jewish reactions and attitudes. The Amsterdam Jews may have had a wonderful life compared to other Jewish communities, but they still had their memories and their bruised feelings and their wariness of possible Gentile attitudes and discriminations. The Amsterdam Jews were not allowed to go to the university and were not citizens and suffered under some legal disabilities. The only time that anything connected to this comes up in the materials we have connected to Spinoza is in a letter of his to his one-time disciple Albert Burgh, who had become a Roman Catholic. Burgh tried to interest his former master in following him into the Church and offered as evidence of the importance of Christian belief that so many have been willing to sacrifice their lives to maintain it in the face of all sorts of persecutions. The discussion of Christian martyrs seems to have touched a raw nerve in Spinoza who, as late as 1675, reacted by telling Burgh about Jewish martyrs, especially one who seems to have made a strong impression on Spinoza, Don Lope de Vera y Alarcon, also known as Judah the Believer.[133] Lope de Vera came from an important Spanish Christian family. He became a Hebrew instructor and more or less converted himself publicly to Judaism. Intense efforts were made by the Church and its inquisitorial officers to get him to renounce his change of religion and to return to the bosom of the Church. He refused and doggedly held his ground until he was finally burned at the stake in 1644. It is reported that as the flames surrounded him at the *auto da fé* he started to sing the hymn that begins "To Thee, O God, I commit my Soul" before he perished. He was a hero to the *marranos* throughout the *marrano* world. Each year on the anniversary of his death there were commemorations in various Sephardic synagogues, including Amsterdam. The story of the martyrdom of Lope de Vera also appears in Menasseh ben Israel's *Hope of Israel* of 1650. Spinoza's strong reaction indicates that there was something still remaining of his original world that came to the surface when Burgh tried to push it aside and replace it with Catholic martyrdom. Since so little of Spinoza's correspondence has survived we do not know if there are other instances of this. The fact that this came up just a couple of years before Spinoza's death suggests that he still possessed some psychological attachment to his Jewish background.

In considering Spinoza both as he saw himself and as a historical figure, we could see that, on the one hand, he is making the most radical, daring move that had occurred in many a century and, on the other, he is obviously building on great ideas set forth most recently by Descartes and Hobbes and, to some extent, by ancient and medieval thinkers, especially of the Neoplatonic variety. Comments that Spinoza made to various people in the early 1660s would indicate that he had pretty much worked out his system by then. He had come to grips with Cartesianism and had moved beyond it. He had found Descartes's dualistic metaphysics incompatible with the monism of a Neoplatonic view of the universe. If God was the ultimate creating and created substance there could be no room for second-order substances that existed independently or apart from God. Hence, the pantheistic system seems to have emerged quite early in Spinoza's life.

In contrast with both Descartes and Hobbes, there seems to be little room for a developmental analysis of Spinoza's philosophy. His two predecessors had started with small works and limited topics, and their efforts took on more and more until they could have a completed philosophy after a decade or two of intellectual struggle. In this, they also profited from knowing what their opponents had to say and being able to guard against it.

Spinoza, we find, tried several ways to put his case forward from about 1661 onward. The unfinished works attest to various plans about how to structure the immense worldview that he was ready to put forth. His correspondence, especially with Oldenburg, indicates a serious desire to refine different points but shows little sign of adding constructions, alterations, or reconsiderations.

Possibly more amazing is that Spinoza by age forty-five had finished his masterpiece. He was concerned to make sure that his masterpiece would be published after his death. As far as we know, he wrote no additional parts to it, or preface, or conclusion, or anything else. He simply and calmly faced the end of his life, interacting with his friends and visitors. Thus, Spinoza was willing to set his masterpiece aside and let people long after him decide if he had really solved the intellectual problems confronting mankind.

Select bibliography

Works by Spinoza

Spinoza Opera. Ed. Carl Gebhardt. 5 vols. Heidelberg: Carl Winter Universitätsverlag, 1972 (1925). The complete works of Spinoza in Latin and Dutch. A late nineteenth-century translation that contains almost all of Spinoza's text is that of R.H.M. Elwes, *The Chief Works of Spinoza*, 2 vols. London: G. Bell, 1883–4. New translations of Spinoza's works by E.M. Curley and Samuel Shirley are valuable in their own ways and should both be consulted and used. E.M. Curley, *The Collected Works of Spinoza*, Princeton: Princeton University Press, 1985 and *Ethics*, London: Penguin Books, 1996. Curley has also edited *A Spinoza reader: the Ethics and other works*, Princeton: Princeton University Press, 1994. A more recent edition of the complete works of Spinoza in English has been translated by Samuel Shirley and edited by Michael Morgan. *Complete Works*, Indianapolis: Hackett, 2002. Shirley, *The Ethics and Selected Letters*, Indianapolis: Hackett, 1982. Very careful annotation by Jacob Adler is included in Shirley's edition of *The Letters*, Indianapolis: Hackett, 1995.

Spinoza's earliest publication?: the Hebrew translation of Margaret Fell's A loving salutation to the seed of

Abraham among the Jews, wherever they are scattered up and down upon the face of the earth, Richard H. Popkin and Michael Signer, eds., Assen, The Netherlands: Van Gorcum, 1987. The Hebrew translation of Margaret Fell's Quaker pamphlet with an introduction by R.H. Popkin. There is some reason to believe that Spinoza worked on this with Samuel Fisher.

Biographies of Spinoza

Pierre Bayle, "Spinoza," *Dictionnaire historique et critique*, Rotterdam: Reinier Leers, 1697. The longest and probably earliest biographical account, of book length, in Bayle's encyclopedic *Dictionnaire*.

Jean Maximilien Lucas and Dominique de Saint-Glain, *La vie de Spinosa*, or *The oldest biography of Spinoza*, trans. Abraham Wolf, Port Washington, NY: Kennikat Press, 1970 (1927). What is called the first biography of Spinoza, attributed to Lucas, is presented in translation here.

Johannes Colerus, *Spinoza, his life and philosophy*, trans. Frederick Pollock, New York: American Scholar Publications, 1699 (1706). Contains the 1705–6 life of Spinoza, *La vie de B. de Spinosa*, by Johann Colerus.

Books and articles about Spinoza

Uriel Acosta. *A Specimen of Human Life*, New York: Bargman, 1967. A moving picture of the fate of the rebel Acosta in 1647.

—— *Examination of Pharisaic traditions = Exame das tradições phariseas*: facsimile of the unique copy in the Royal Library of Copenhagen, trans. and ed. H.P. Salomon, I.S.D. Sassoon, and Semuel da Silva, Leiden: Brill, 1993. A long-lost statement of the views of the leading rebel in the Jewish community before Spinoza.

Wiep van Bunge, *From Stevin to Spinoza: an essay on philosophy in the seventeenth-century Dutch Republic*, Leiden:

Brill, 2001. An important study that places Spinoza in the context of Dutch thought of the time.

E.M. Curley and Pierre-François Moreau, eds., *Spinoza: issues and directions*: the proceedings of the Chicago Spinoza Conference, Leiden, Brill, 1990. The publication of the papers given at a major conference about Spinoza which has since launched many investigations.

Alan Donagan, *Spinoza*, Chicago: University of Chicago Press, 1989. An important study of Spinoza's metaphysics.

Lewis Feuer, *Spinoza and the Rise of Liberalism*, Boston: Beacon Press, 1958. A provocative study of Spinoza's possible role in liberal politics in seventeenth-century Holland.

Jacob Freudenthal, *Spinoza: Sein Leben und Seine Lehre*, Heidelberg: C. Winter, 1927. A fundamental nineteenth-century study which published for the first time the full text of the excommunication (*herem*) and the contents of Spinoza's library, among many other things.

Don Garrett, *The Cambridge companion to Spinoza*, Cambridge: Cambridge University Press, 1996. A collection of studies by leading authorities on different aspects of Spinoza.

Marjorie Glicksman Grene, *Spinoza, a collection of critical essays*, Garden City, NY: Anchor Books, 1973. A collection of studies, mostly concerning Spinoza's relation to the science of his time.

Stuart Hampshire, *Spinoza*, London: Faber and Faber, 1956. A lively account of Spinoza's theories by a leading English contemporary philosopher.

Jonathan I. Israel, *Radical Enlightenment: philosophy and the making of modernity*, 1650–1750, Oxford: Oxford University Press, 2001. A recent ground-breaking study offering a new theory about Spinoza's early roots in Cartesian thought and his influence on the European radical Enlightenment.

Yosef Kaplan, *From Christianity to Judaism: the Story of Isaac Orobio de Castro*, Oxford: Oxford University Press, 1989. One of the very best studies of what the Jewish community was like at

Spinoza's time and afterwards told as a biography of the most important intellectual in the group after Spinoza.

Asa Kasher and Shlomo Biderman, "Why was Baruch de Spinoza Excommunicated?," *Sceptics, Millenarians and Jews,* ed. David S. Katz and Jonathan I. Israel, Leiden: Brill, 1990. A lengthy exploration of various theories that might explain why Spinoza was excommunicated.

Leszek Kolakowski, *Chrétiens sans église: la conscience religeuse et le lien confessionnel au XVIIe siècle,* Paris: Gallimard, 1969. A study of the radical leaning millenarian reformers, especially in the Netherlands, with whom Spinoza was associated for most of his lifetime.

Henry Méchoulan, *Amsterdam au temps de Spinoza: argent et liberté,* Paris: PUF, 1990. A study of what members of the Jewish community at Spinoza's time might have made of the issues that bothered the young philosopher that has not yet, unfortunately, been translated into English.

Steven M. Nadler, *Spinoza: a life,* Cambridge: Cambridge University Press, 1999. A recent biography that tries to take account of much of the new information about Spinoza's life and activities.

Richard H. Popkin, *The History of Scepticism: from Savonarola to Bayle,* Oxford: Oxford University Press, 2003. Revised and expanded edition that includes a chapter on Spinoza's reaction to skeptical currents in philosophical thought.

Heidi M. Ravven and Lenn Evan Goodman, *Jewish themes in Spinoza's philosophy,* Albany: SUNY Press, 2002. A collection of essays by different scholars on a wide range of topics.

I.S. Révah, *Spinoza et le Dr. Juan de Prado,* Paris: Mouton, 1959. A study which revealed that Spinoza had a comrade in the synagogue in his avant-garde ideas.

Daniel Swetschinski, *Reluctant Cosmopolitans: the Portuguese Jews of seventeenth-century Amsterdam,* London: Littman Library of Jewish Civilization, 2000. A fundamental study of the social and economic background of the leading figures of the Spanish Portuguese synagogue in Amsterdam.

Harry Austryn Wolfson, *The philosophy of Spinoza: unfolding the latent processes of his reasoning*, Cambridge: Harvard University Press, 1983. A monumental study of the roots of Spinoza's thought in medieval Jewish philosophy.

Yirmiahu Yovel, *Spinoza and Other Heretics*, Princeton: Princeton University Press, 1989. An attempt to portray Spinoza in terms of the *marrano* world of the time.

Notes

1. Harry Austryn Wolfson, *The philosophy of Spinoza: Unfolding the latent processes of his reasoning* (Cambridge: Harvard University Press, 1983).

2. See Pierre Bayle, article "Spinoza," *Dictionnaire historique et critique* (Rotterdam: Reinier Leers, 1697); Pierre Bayle, Francis Halma, and Isaac Jaquelot, *Het leven van B. de Spinoza: met eenige aanteekeningen over zyn bedryf, schriften, en gevoelens* (Utrecht: Halma, 1698).

3. Jean-Maximilien Lucas and Dominique de Saint-Glain, *La vie de Spinosa* (Hambourg, Kunrath, 1735); see also Lucas and Saint-Glain, *The oldest biography of Spinoza*, A. Wolf, ed. (Port Washington, NY: Kennikat Press, 1927, 1970 reprint).

4. Johannes Colerus, *La vie de B. de Spinosa, tirée des écrits de ce fameux philosohe, et du témoignage de plusieurs persones dignes de foi, qui l'ont connu particuliérement* (La Haye: Chez T. Johnson, Machand Libraire, 1706).

5. On *marranos*, see *Des marranes à Spinoza*, ed. I.S. Révah, Henry Méchoulan, and P.-F. Moreau (Paris: J. Vrin, 1995).

6. Jonathan Israel, *The Dutch Republic: its rise, greatness and fall*, 1477–1806 (Oxford: Clarendon Press, 1995); Herbert Rowen, *The princes of Orange: the stadholders in the Dutch Republic* (Cambridge: Cambridge University Press, 1988).

7. G.B. Stouppe, *La religion des Hollandois: representée en plusieurs lettres écrites par un officier de l'armée du Roy, à un pasteur & professeur en theologie de Berne* (Paris: F. Clousier, 1673).

8. Israel, *The Dutch Republic*.

9. Richard H. Popkin, "Hartlib, Dury and the Jews," *Samuel Hartlib & Universal Reformation: Studies in Intellectual Communication*, ed. Mark Greengrass, Michael Leslie, and Timothy Raylor (Cambridge: Cambridge University Press, 1994), pp. 118–136.

10. See Daniel Swetschinski, *Reluctant cosmopolitans: the Portuguese Jews of seventeenth-century Amsterdam* (London: Littman Library of Jewish Civilization, 2000), pp. 12–14.

11. Grotius was a leader of the moderate Calvinist faction, called the Arminians, who were outvoted at the Synod of Dordrecht. Some of the top figures in the group were arrested and beheaded by the victorious orthodox Calvinist faction. It is reported that Grotius only survived because he was hidden in a trunk and carried out of the country. He went on to Paris where he became the Swedish ambassador there.

12. It is not known how the work got from Lithuania to Amsterdam or why a Caraite author would be so acceptable to a Sephardic Jewish audience. The Caraites were a Jewish heretical group, which in the eighth and ninth centuries insisted on *only* studying the biblical text without any reliance on rabbinical tradition or other source material. They were Jewish fundamentalists before there was any fundamentalism. They created sufficient disruption in Jewish communities that the dominant rabbinical authorities expelled them and had them banned from being part of the Jewish world from then on. They managed to survive in various places, such as Lithuania, the Crimea, Egypt, and Constantinople, and even exist today, but they are still not recognized as part of the Jewish world. See Richard H. Popkin, "Reason as the Rule of Faith in Castellio, the Early Socinians and the Jews," *Aequitas, Aequalitas, Auctoritas: Theoretical Reason and Legitimation of*

Authority in XVIth Century Europe, ed. Danièle Letocha (Paris: J. Vrin, 1992), pp. 195–203.

13.   The manuscripts were carefully written out, looking almost like medieval manuscripts. Some of them have the name of the scribe on them. There are a large number of these from the late 1620s into the early nineteenth century. This seems to have been a favorite polemic. It was published in Hebrew at the end of the seventeenth century by the German theologian Johann Christophe Wagenseil as an example of how much the Jews hate the Christians.

14.   This may be because, although it circulated freely, there is no sign that it really came to the attention of Christian authors until 1715 when copies of it were auctioned off in the sale of the library of the son-in-law of the French Huguenot theologian and historian Jacques Basnages. From then on, it turns up in eighteenth-century Enlightenment discussions. Attempts to refute it appear in England in the 1840s and it was still being discussed in German academies just before the time of Hitler. So, it has had a long life though it has hardly been taken seriously in mainline Jewish discussions outside of Amsterdam. An abbreviated version was printed in the United States translated by Trude-Weiss Rosmarin (New York: Ktav, 1970).

15.   Marc Saperstein, "Christianity, Christians, and 'New Christians' in Morteira's Sermons," *HUCA*, 170–71 (1999–2000), 329–84.

16.   I.S. Révah, *Spinoza et le Dr. Juan de Prado* (Paris: Mouton, 1959) and "Aux origines de la rupture spinozienne: Nouveaux documents sur l'incroyance dans la communauté Judeo-Portuguese d'Amsterdam à l'èpoque de l'excommunication de Spinoza," *Revue des Etudes Juives*, cxxiii (1964), pp. 359–431. See also Yosef Kaplan, *From Christianity to Judaism. The Story of Orobio de Castro* (Oxford: Oxford University Press, 1989), pp. 123–60. In writing their anti-Christian works, Orobio and d'Aguilar went back to the first Christian apologetics by Spanish New Christians like Pablo de Santa Maria and took on several

more sixteenth-century Spanish and Italian Christian controversialists. There are some other lengthy anti-Christian manuscripts by Gomes de Silvera and Isaac Naar. Some other items are listed by Jacques Basnage as having been in the collection of his son-in-law, including anti-Christian works by Rabbi Judah Leon Templo, Rabbi Menasseh ben Israel, among others.

17. See Adam Sutcliffe, *Judaism and Enlightenment* (Cambridge: Cambridge University Press, 2003).

18. Saperstein, "Christianity, Christians, and 'New Christians,'" 334–5.

19. Presently, there are three known copies, which all seem to come from Menasseh's original. One is at the William Andrews Clark library at UCLA. A study of it by some experts came to the conclusion it was written in Italy in the 1630s but nothing more seems to be known about it. We do not know how Menasseh came to have a copy or why he took it to England with him.

20. Swetschinski, *Reluctant Cosmopolitans*, 83–4.

21. See Jacob Freudenthal, *Spinoza, sein leben und seine lehre* (Heidelberg: C. Winter, 1927).

22. Wolfson, *The philosophy of Spinoza*; Warren Harvey, "Hasdai Crescas, Joseph Albo, and Isaac Abrabanel," *The Pimlico History of Western Philosophy* (London: Pimlico, 1999), pp. 204–10.

23. Jonathan Israel, *Radical Enlightenment* (Oxford: Oxford University Press, 2001), pp. 168–9.

24. See Popkin, *Isaac La Peyrère (1596–1676): his life, work, and influence* (Leiden: Brill, 1987).

25. H.P. Salomon, introduction to *Examination of Pharisaic traditions = Exame das tradições phariseas*: facsimile of the unique copy in the Royal Library of Copenhagen (Leiden: Brill, 1993).

26. Philip van Limborch and Orobio de Castro, *Philippi a Limborch De veritate religionis christianae amica collatio cum erudito Judaeo* (Basle: J.R. Imhoff, 1740). The autobiographical fragment, found in papers of Limborch's father-in-law, was added by van Limborch to show how bad Jews can be. This

debate was republished a few times. It was apparently a genuinely public debate and a significant intellectual event at which, among others, John Locke was present. Locke wrote a long review of it for Jean Leclerc's *Bibliothèque ancienne et moderne*. It would be interesting to find out who else was present and whether the case of Da Costa was discussed apart from the actual debate. There are several letters of Locke to Limborch about the debate. Perhaps there are some, as yet unfound, items in Locke's papers relating to the Da Costa manuscript.

27.   See Orobio de Castro, *Certamen Philosophicum, Propugnatae Veritatis Divinae ac Naturalis adversus Joh. Bredenburg* (Amsterdam, 1703).

28.   See Salomon, *Examination of Pharisaic traditions*. I was expressing my doubts about the authenticity of the Da Costa autobiography when Herman P. Salomon announced that he had discovered the first known copy of Da Costa's book *Exame das tradições phariseas*. Although all copies were supposedly destroyed at the time he was first excommunicated, Salomon had found a copy bound with something else in the Royal Library of Copenhagen. This text has been edited and now is available for anyone to study. It is an exciting rebellious text a bit in advance of its time. At the time of Salomon's discovery, I was asked by a journalist about its significance and I said it depends on who read it and who was influenced by it. If literally nobody read it until Salomon found it then it is an unimportant piece of the past that reveals nothing about how radical religious ideas developed. It is just a curiosity unless it can be shown to be a part of the developing critiques of religion of the time.

29.   Steven Nadler, *Spinoza: A Life* (Cambridge: Cambridge University Press, 1999).

30.   See Bayle, article "Spinoza," *Dictionnaire historique et critique* (Rotterdam: Reinier Leers, 1697) and *Historical and Critical Dictionary, Selections*, ed. Richard H. Popkin (Indianapolis: Hackett, 1991); see also Colerus, *La vie de B. de Spinosa*.

31. Richard H. Popkin, "Spinoza's Excommunication," *Jewish Themes in Spinoza's Philosophy*, ed. Heidi Ravven and Lenn Goodman (Albany, NY: State University of New York Press, 2002).

32. Kaplan, *From Christianity to Judaism*.

33. Salomon, introduction to *Examination of Pharisaic traditions*.

34. Révah, *Spinoza et le Dr. Juan de Prado*; Popkin, *Isaac La Peyrère*.

35. Kaplan, *From Christianity to Judaism*.

36. See Asa Kasher and Shlomo Biderman, "Why was Baruch de Spinoza Excommunicated?," *Sceptics, Millenarians and Jews*, ed. David S. Katz and Jonathan I. Israel (Leiden: Brill, 1990), pp. 98–141; Israel, *Radical Enlightenment*, 169–70.

37. Odette Vlessing, "The Excommunication of Baruch Spinoza: The Birth of a Philosopher."

38. Lewis Feuer, *Spinoza and the Rise of Liberalism* (Boston: Beacon Press, 1958).

39. See Richard H. Popkin, "Jewish Messianism and Christian Millenarianism," *Culture and Politics from Puritanism to the Enlightenment*, ed. Perez Zagorin (Berkeley: University of California Press, 1980), pp. 67–90.

40. Richard H. Popkin, "Jewish Christian Relations in the 16th and 17th Century: The Conception of the Messiah," *Jewish History*, Vol. 6, 1992, pp. 163–77; "The first college for Jewish studies," *Revue des études juives*, Vol. 143, no. 3–4 (July–December 1984); and "Hartlib, Dury and the Jews," 118–36; see also Leszek Kolakowski, *Chrétiens sans église: la conscience religeuse et le lien confessionnel au XVIIe siècle* (Paris: Gallimard, 1969).

41. Richard H. Popkin, "Spinoza, the Quakers, and the Millenarians, 1656–1658," *Manuscrito*, Vol. 6, 1982, pp. 113–33; Ernestine van der Wall, *De mystieke chiliast Petrus Serrarius 1600–1669 en zijn wereld* (Leiden: van der Wall, 1987).

42. Richard H. Popkin, "Spinoza and Samuel Fisher," *Philosophia: philosophical quarterly of Israel*, Vol. 15, no. 3 (December 1985).

43.   Richard H. Popkin, "Rabbi Nathan Shapira's Visit to Amsterdam in 1657," *Dutch Jewish History* (Jerusalem: Tel-Aviv University, 1984).

44.   Theo Verbeek, *La Querelle d'Utrecht: René Descartes et Martin Schoock* (Paris: Impressions nouvelles, 1988).

45.   See Kasher and Biderman, "Why was Baruch de Spinoza Excommunicated?"

46.   Josef Penso de la Vega, *Confusion de confusions: dialogos curiosos entre un philosopho agudo, un mercador discreto, y un accionista erudito descriviendo el negocio de las acciones, su origen, su ethimologia, su realidad, su juego, y su enredo* (Amsterdam, 1688).

47.   Vlessing, "The Excommunication of Baruch Spinoza."

48.   Israel, *Radical Enlightenment*, 165–7.

49.   Nadler, *Spinoza*; Kaplan, *From Christianity to Judaism*; Richard H. Popkin, "The Banning of Spinoza: Was it a major or minor event in 1656?," paper given at a conference on Spinoza entitled "After Spinoza: Judaism, Modernity, and the Future of the Multitude" at UCLA, Center for Jewish Studies, February 9–11, 2003.

50.   Jacques Basnage, *Histoire des Juifs* (The Hague: H. Scheurleer, 1716).

51.   John Selden, *The historie of tithes, that is, the practice of payment of them, the positiue laws made for them, the opinions touching the right of them: a review of it is also annext, which both confirmes it and directs in the use of it* (London: s.n., 1618).

52.   Freudenthal, *Spinoza: Sein Leben und seine Lehre*.

53.   Ibid.

54.   Van der Wall, *De mystieke chiliast Petrus Serrarius*.

55.   See Kolakowski, *Chrétiens sans église*.

56.   Popkin, "Spinoza and Samuel Fisher."

57.   See Richard H. Popkin, "Spinoza's Relations with the Quakers," *Quaker History*, Vol. 70, 1984, pp. 14–28.

58.   Révah, *Spinoza et le Dr. Juan de Prado*.

59.   On Spinoza and Van den Enden, see Israel, *Radical Enlightenment*, 168–9, 171.

60.   See letter from Oldenburg to Spinoza, Ep 79, 11 February 1676, *The Letters*, ed. Samuel Shirley, Steven Barbone, Lee Rice, and Jacob Adler (Indianapolis: Hackett, 1995), 347–8.

61.   Letter from Oldenburg to Spinoza, Ep 33, 8 December 1665, *The Letters*, 199–200.

62.   On Sabbatai Zevi, see Gershom Scholem, *Sabbatai Sevi: The Mystical Messiah*, 1626–1676 (Princeton: Princeton University Press, 1973).

63.   In fact, there is a gap of several years in his correspondence with Oldenburg starting at this point. One of the principal reasons for this pause in correspondence was the fact that Oldenburg was arrested for being involved with suspicious foreigners and seems to have become very guarded in his correspondence over the next few years. Some time in the early 1670s, however, he resumes his communication with Spinoza.

64.   Letter of Serrarius to Oldenburg, 5 July 1667. See Oldenburg, *Correspondence* (Madison: University of Wisconsin Press, 1965).

65.   Spinoza, *Tractatus Theologico-Politicus*, ed. Samuel Shirley (Leiden: Brill, 1989), 101.

66.   Spinoza, *The Principles of the Philosophy of René Descartes* in *Earlier Philosophical Writings*, trans. Frank A. Hayes (Indianapolis: 1963), 13.

67.   Ibidem.

68.   Ibid., 17.

69.   Ibid., 20.

70.   Ibid., 33.

71.   Ibid., Part 1, props. 13 and 14.

72.   *On the Improvement of the Understanding* (New York: 1955), Vol. 2, 17.

73.   Ibidem.

74.   Ibid., 30.

75.   Ibid., 11–12.

76.   Israel, *Radical Enlightenment*, 246–9.

77.   Feuer, *Spinoza and the Rise of Liberalism*. Much has been written about the possible relations between Spinoza and De Witt,

ranging from claims that Spinoza was the brains behind De Witt's liberalism, to claims that De Witt was financially supporting Spinoza because of Spinoza's innovative ideas. Though Spinoza and De Witt had several mutual friends and acquaintances, no actual evidence of a relationship has been found. Herbert Rowen, who did an exhaustive study of De Witt's papers, said there was nothing in them connecting the two persons. Even so, there has been a rumor of a connection from the time when they were both alive down to the present. In the last few years, one item has been found indicating that De Witt refused to let Spinoza meet him because he did not want to be seen with the person who had written the *Tractatus*. Therefore, in spite of the romantic claims about Spinoza and De Witt, I think one has to remain somewhat skeptical until some evidence is found of any actual relationship. See Rowen, *John de Witt, grand pensionary of Holland*, 1625–1672 (Princeton, NJ: Princeton University Press, 1978). See also, Israel, *Radical Enlightenment*, 278.

78. *TTP*, 6.
79. Ibid., 76.
80. Ibid., chap. 3, 56.
81. Popkin, "Rabbi Nathan Shapira's Visit to Amsterdam."
82. *TTP*, chap. 14, 187.
83. *TTP*, chap. 4, 59.
84. Popkin, "Spinoza and Samuel Fisher."
85. *TTP*, chap. 17.
86. Jean Calvin, *Institutes of the Christian Religion* (Philadelphia: Westminster Press, 1960).
87. Richard Simon, *Histoire critique du Vieux Testament* (Paris?, 1678).
88. Henry Méchoulan, *Amsterdam au temps de Spinoza: argent et liberté* (Paris: Presses universitaires de France, 1990).
89. Israel, *Radical Enlightenment*, 275–84.
90. For More, see Popkin, *History of Scepticism*, 175–80, 213–5 and "Cudworth," *The Third Force in Seventeenth-Century Thought* (Leiden: Brill, 1992).

91.   *Ethics*, ed. Samuel Shirley (Indianapolis: Hackett, 1982), 39–40.

92.   See Franz Hartmann, *The life and Doctrine of Jacob Boehme, the God-Taught philosopher* (Boston: The Occult publishing company, 1891); and Alexandre Koyré, *La Philosophie de Jacob Boehme* (Paris: J. Vrin, 1929).

93.   *TTP*, chap. 9, 125.

94.   Ibidem.

95.   Johann Georg Wachter, *Der Spinozismus im Jüdenthumb* (1699) (Stuttgart-Bad Cannstatt: Frommann-Holzboog, 1994); Basnage, *Histoire des Juifs*.

96.   *Ethics*, 31.

97.   *Ethics*, Axiom 6, 32.

98.   Ibid., 63.

99.   Ibid., 66.

100.   See the recent work by Antonio Damasio, *Looking for Spinoza: joy, sorrow, and the feeling brain* (Orlando, FL: Harcourt, 2003), who found that Spinoza's double-aspect theory, that modes can be conceived in terms of extension or in terms of ideas, best fits with the growing evidence from neurophysiology of how the mind/brain interacts in human experience. This may yield important new understandings of human nature in the near future.

101.   *Ethics*, 61.

102.   Ibid., 62.

103.   Ibid., 63. My italics.

104.   Ibid., 225.

105.   Letter from Burgh to Spinoza, 3 September 1675, *Letters*, 303–4.

106.   Spinoza to Burgh, December 1675, ibid., 342.

107.   *Ethics*, 66.

108.   Yirmiahu Yovel, *Spinoza and Other Heretics* (Princeton: Princeton University Press, 1989).

109.   Leo Strauss, *Persecution and the Art of Writing* (Glencoe: Free Press, 1952).

110. Israel, *Radical Enlightenment*, 285–94.

111. Milan's father-in-law, Rabbi Benjamin Musafia, was a well-known figure among the Amsterdam Jews. Milan himself became the Danish governor of the Virgin Islands and long after his acquaintance with Spinoza, Milan was arrested, tried, and executed by the Danish government for treason and fraud. On Milan, Spinoza, and the case of the army officer, see Michael Petry and Guido Suchtelen, "Spinoza and the Military: A Newly Discovered Document," *Studia Spinoza*, I (1985), 359–69.

112. Israel, *Radical Enlightenment*, 505–6.

113. Colonel Stouppe, in 1655, was the Reverend J.-B. Stouppe of the French Reformed Church in London and a chief intelligence officer for Oliver Cromwell. It was Stouppe who was given the task of trying to arouse a revolution on the part of the French Protestants and get them to accept the prince of Condé as their king. We know that Stouppe brought a message across Europe to The Hague where the prince was then in residence, offering him the crown of France if he would start the rebellion. The prince, for better or worse, said he would start the rebellion *the day after* Cromwell invaded France. A complete realignment of European parties almost took place in 1655. Thereafter, the prince of Condé became a loyal commander of the French army under Louis XIV and Stouppe was forced into exile with the end of the Puritan Revolution. He ceased being a minister and became a military person and stayed with Condé for many years. Later on, Stouppe was forced to leave France at the time of the revocation of the Edict of Nantes and, along with his friend Gilbert Burnet, made a famous voyage to Rome and then to the Netherlands where they became part of the entourage of William of Orange in 1688–9. On Stouppe, see Popkin, "The First Published Reaction to Spinoza's *Tractatus*: Col. J.B. Stouppe, the Condé Circle, and the Rev. Jean Lebrun," *The Spinozistic Heresy*, pp. 6–12.

114. On Condé, see Popkin, "Serendipity at the Clark," *Clark Newsletter*, no. 16, 1986, 5.

115.   A French pastor, Jean Le Brun, who seemed to know Spinoza, criticized Stouppe and mentioned that it was Stouppe who made the arrangements.

116.   Ibidem. The duc d'Aumale, who became the inheritor of the Condé palace and archives at Chantilly, said, in his seven-volume history of the prince, that Spinoza had come to visit the prince when the prince was indisposed in Utrecht. They had many conversations, which the prince enjoyed, and the prince invited him to come to France with him, an invitation that Spinoza declined. The only source given for this is the archives of the prince of Condé at Chantilly without any specific page reference. The archives are enormous and, as yet, far from being completely indexed, so it is not possible to check out this information.

117.   Bayle, *Oeuvres diverses* (The Hague: Husson, Johnson, 1727–31), 872.

118.   Morelli's relations with Spinoza first appear in Saint-Évremond's poems published in England by Pierre Desmaizeaux, a Huguenot refugee who was a close friend of Pierre Bayle. Of Morelli, Saint-Évremond wrote:

> Seven Cities, you know, contended for the birth of HOMER: seven great Nations contended for that of MORELLI; India, Egypt, Arabia, Persia, Turkey, Italy, and Spain. The cold Countries, nay even the temperate; France, England, Germany, have no manner of pretension to it. He understands all the Languages, and speaks most of them. His elevated, majestick, and figurative stile, makes me think he was born in the East, and that he has learnt all the best things that are among the Europeans. He loves Musick passionately, and Poetry to distraction: in Painting, he is curios, at least; but whether he is a Connoisseur, I know not: as to Architecture, he has friends who understand it: he is seriously famous for his profession, and capable of exercising that of others.

See Quentin M. Hope, *Saint Evremond and His Friends* (Geneva: Droz, 1999), p. 283.

119.   A possible influence of Morelli's in this regard may be the views expressed by the earl of Rochester before his deathbed

conversion. The account we have of the conversion written by Gilbert Burnet portrays the earl as tormented by his libertine life and by the spinozistic implications of his world outlook. As he struggles with this he is finally brought by Burnet to rejoin Christianity just before he expired. Of course, we only have Burnet's version.

120.   Bayle, article "Spinoza," *Dictionnaire.*

121.   Richard H. Popkin, "Another Spinoza?," *Journal of the History of Philosophy,* 34: 1 January 1996, 133.

122.   Boxel to Spinoza, Ep 51, 14 September 1674, *Letters,* 261; Spinoza to Boxel, Ep 52, September 1674, *Letters,* 262–3; Burgh to Spinoza Ep 67, 3 September 1675, *Letters,* 303–12; Spinoza to Burgh, Ep 76, n.d., *Letters,* 340–44.

123.   Jonathan Israel has found much spinozistic material coming out of left-leaning theologians in the Netherlands, England, Germany, France, and Scandinavia. Spinoza's ideas were taken over and applied to religious issues of the time. See *Radical Enlightenment,* Part 5, 563–720.

124.   Orobio de Castro, *Réfutation des erreurs de Benoit Spinosa* (Brussels: F. Foppens, 1731).

125.   David Hume, *A Treatise of Human Nature,* ed. David Fate Norton and Mary J. Norton, Book 1, Part 4, Sections 5–6 (Oxford: Oxford University Press, 2000).

126.   Chevalier Ramsay, *The philosophical principles of natural and revealed religion, unfolded in a geometrical order* (Glasgow: R. Foulis, 1748–9).

127.   Alan Kors, *Atheism in France,* 1650–1729 (Princeton: Princeton University Press, 1990).

128.   See Israel, *Radical Enlightenment,* 566–8, 570, 584–5, 586–90, 684–92.

129.   Popkin, "*The Age of Reason* and *The Age of Revelation*: Two Critics of Tom Paine: David Levi and Elias Boudinot," *Deism, Masonry and the Enlightenment. Essays Honoring Alfred Owen Aldridge,* ed. J.A.L. Lemay (Newark, DE, University of Delaware Press, 1987), 158–70.

130.   The only known copy of the 1719 printing is in the Spinoza collection at UCLA. This was discovered by Sylvia Berti in 1982.

131.   Coleridge, *Biographia Literaria* (Oxford: The Clarendon Press, 1907).

132.   Adam Sutcliffe, "Spinoza and Friends: Judaism, Christianity and the Spirit of Philosophy in the Berlin 'Spinoza Quarrel' and Since," 8–13. Paper given at the conference *After Spinoza: Judaism, Modernity, and the Future of the Multitude*, UCLA Center for Jewish Studies, February 9–11, 2003.

133.   Letter from Spinoza to Burgh, Ep 76, *Letters*, 343.

Index